SELF-HYPNOSIS IN TWO DAYS

SELF-HYPNOSIS
IN TWO DAYS

Freda Morris

A Dutton  *Paperback*

E. P. DUTTON NEW YORK

Originally Published by Intergalactic Publishing Co., 1974.
This paperback edition of *Self-Hypnosis in Two Days*
first published by E. P. Dutton & Co., Inc. in 1975

First Edition

10   9   8   7   6   5   4

Published simultaneously in Canada
by Clarke, Irwin & Company Limited, Toronto and Vancouver
ISBN: 0-525-47403-x

Library of Congress Catalog Card Number: 75-13982

ACKNOWLEDGMENTS

The author would like to express her appreciation to all the people
from the Chateau and its networks.

DRAWINGS BY THE AUTHOR

Contents

Preface*

Before this book was published by E. P. Dutton and Company I published it myself. The way I became the Intergalactic Publishing Company seems very odd. Three years ago I was a professor of medical psychology at UCLA Medical School. After the repressive attitudes toward hypnosis and psychic phenomena I had been subjected to in the Midwest, this position in California where I could teach hypnosis and find support for my psychic interests seemed perfect. I loved the incredible amount of freedom I had. It reminded me of my free-roaming childhood in the southeastern Oklahoma woods.

Then through a series of events I was convinced that I could have still more freedom if I gave up all

* This Preface is expanded from an article in the magazine *The Self-Publishing Writer* and appears here by permission of the publisher.

7

power relationships. A power relationship is any relationship in which one person holds a threat (in our society, usually withdrawal of material goods) over another and can thus force that person to do things he wouldn't otherwise do.

The contact which led to my interest in this began with a misplaced phone call from an architecture professor.

"You have the wrong number," I said. "But it wouldn't do any good if you got the right one because Dr. Moss is on leave of absence. Maybe I can help you. We do about the same kind of work."

The man came to my office that afternoon to discuss his psychic unfoldment. In the process he told of a former classmate who was living in a commune in Virginia, traveling with some other commune members, and spreading a "let things happen as they may" philosophy which had helped the professor accept his psychic experiences.

For some reason that didn't make too much logical sense I insisted on meeting these people immediately. The professor called someone who told him they were at a nearby beach. He gave me directions and said I could recognize them since one was a young Allen Ginsberg, one a curly-haired Tarzan, and the woman looked like Mona Lisa. I located them easily and found them eager to tell their story.

They were members of a community started twenty years ago by a Virginia man who had overcome his redneck heritage and become a sort of Zen master without portfolio. They described him as a person who

rarely spoke unless spoken to but who was very articulate in explaining the no-power relationship philosophy he espouses.

Within a month I took my children and went to Virginia on vacation. After talking for five days with this Virginian in a totally free-form community where there were no duties, no schedules—nothing to interfere with the moment-to-moment ability to follow one's intuition—I was convinced that I wasn't as free as I had thought. He explained that in power relationships both parties are limited and unable to follow their intuitions.

When I asked him how I could achieve more freedom, he answered that my biggest step would be to free my children from the parent-child power relationship. I could accomplish this by giving them everything I owned and never giving them any more orders, suggestions, or advice unless they asked.

Giving up the power of the pocketbook over my

children might lead to some interesting changes, though I didn't expect anything drastic. I thought they were already very free children and were doing pretty much what they wanted.

On March 15, 1971, I told them they could have everything I owned. They accepted unbelievingly. This gift included several thousand dollars in money, a house with pool and big mortgage, a car, forty acres of land, furniture, books, clothes, and personal effects. I assumed they would go on living with me wherever I went, but once they had their own power they also had minds of their own.

The boy, who was twelve and a half, bought his sister's share of the house and after spending the summer in Europe started a Summerhill boardinghouse, of sorts, and got himself into a Summerhill school not far from the house.

He is sixteen now and is still living there with enough people to meet the payments and expenses. After a couple of years of focus on emotional growth (commonly called goofing off) at Summerhill, he seemed to have a yen for academia again. He found a well-organized, high-standards private school where he started out majoring in paramedical education. He said he would have a big-paying job in emergency medical care by the time he was eighteen. He worked parttime in a convalescent hospital for awhile, but the last I heard he had changed to electronics and had started a business in his house.

The girl, who was sixteen, helped start a farm commune in Oregon. After a year or so she and the leader of the commune decided they wanted a family and business of their own, *sans* commune. Now they they have a shoe factory and a beautiful baby boy in a small city in California.

She bought her brother's share of the forty acres, which is in Oklahoma, and is having a house built on it. They plan to sell their factory in a year or so and become lady and gentleman farmers with hired hands.

"It will be a little like the commune except we can hire and fire," she explained.

Looks like rebellion against my "no-power relationship" stance. I love the beautiful contrast and the surprises. If I had been "guiding" my children I could never have come up with the ideas they have. My relationships with both of them have grown progressively more idyllic since I made my decision to give them freedom *and* resources.

The next step in freeing myself was to get rid of the employer-employee relationship. I took a year's leave from UCLA and went to the Virginia community to learn some more about following one's intuition.

Since I'd given everything away and only worked long enough to get a back-pack, some traveling clothes, and a little expense money, I could only afford to travel by hitchhiking.

After spending a few months in Virginia, hitching back and forth across the country a few times and having many interesting adventures, I met a man in Berkeley with whom it was a challenge to develop a no-power relationship. He is an old-fashioned, no-nonsense doctor who really turns me on. Getting the

concept of a no-power relationship across to him took most of my energy for several months, but it was energy well spent.

When the relationship with him settled into relative "nuptial" bliss, I channeled part of my energy into finding ways to express my creative outbursts and make money without slipping back into power relationships with employers and patients. I was trained as a psychotherapist, and what could be more power-oriented than a traditional therapist-patient relationship? Psychotherapy was my field though, and I hoped in private practice somehow to obviate the power aspects.

I tried having my patients pay what the treatment was actually worth. The price of a pack of cigarettes a day when you quit smoking, for instance, or so much a pound for the fat you lose and keep off. How much is it worth to get rid of your phobia so you can fly? To pass your bar exam so you can practice law? To overcome impotence? To stop drinking? To get rid of hay fever?

People just couldn't, wouldn't handle the responsibility of deciding how to pay and how much to pay. The fat woman has been hiding her thin frame from me ever since. The smoker was overwhelmed at the thousands of dollars a couple of packs a day add up to. The others insisted on paying each session. So for a while I went back into the thirty dollar an hour racket.

Several things were wrong: (1) I was disappointed that I couldn't get psychotherapy going on a contractual basis. (2) Even though I had done a lot to reduce the power plays in my therapeutic dealings by showing my patients how to hypnotize themselves and insisting they take their own power, I was still their doctor with power over them. And I was also their employee, in a sense, paid by the hour. (3) Thirty dollars seemed like a rip-off at sessions where I wasn't innovative and the patient didn't have some kind of breakthrough. (4) I had to make appointments so couldn't follow my intuition about what I wanted to do moment to moment. (5) Worst of all, I wasn't improving as a therapist. I seemed to have reached a plateau in therapeutic competence.

It was this last dissatisfaction, the lack of growth, that turned the tide for me. I had wanted to be a writer before I wanted to be a psychologist and somehow priority seemed important. At sixteen I planned to be a writer, at seventeen, a psychologist. After all the exciting experiences of the past couple of years I had plenty to write about. And there was certainly room for competence building in this field where I was inexperienced and untrained. I slacked off my practice and began to spend more and more time writing.

When I decided to be a writer I started by producing an opus called *The Hitchhiking Hypnotist: An Autobiographical Adventure*. Writing it was a good way to get experience, but unfortunately, when I finished it, it lacked many qualities that make a book.

I paused and gave the whole thing some more thought. I had studied for years and years to become a good therapist. Maybe doing therapy didn't come as naturally as it seemed and I *had* learned something useful in those years of study. Obviously writing an adventure story took some know-how I didn't have.

I asked myself, "What do I know so well that I could write it in my sleep? What personal experience have I had which would be of value to others? What could I write that would be themeless, character developmentless, and free of all those other writer things I have not yet learned about? What would have a clearcut market?"

"I know hypnosis forward and backward," I answered. "My experience with self-hypnosis as a student leaves no doubt of its value since I had been an ordinary student before I learned it but afterward made straight A's. And since then I have used it to meet almost every challenge that I have faced."

So I came up with *Self-Hypnosis in Two Days*. The market was clearly people who take exams or want to meet other challenges successfully. And to make it easy to avoid power relationships in this venture I had a friend who wanted to start a "How to—" publishing house. She suggested I get it all down in first draft and let her worry about the editing.

I laid *The Hitchhiking Hypnotist* and my other grandiose projects aside and took a few weeks to write this book. After a little editing, it looked good enough for some trial runs. My publisher planned to give copies to some people who were interested in going through the weekend program. With that settled I left for London, expecting to come back, interview the people who had spent the weekend with the book, revise it based on their experiences, and have it ready for my publisher again a few weeks after I returned.

My old-fashioned, no-nonsense doctor (who is, nevertheless, very interested in psychic research) and I did a personally designed psychic tour of England and Scotland. While we were gone my publisher friend, who had been tending in the direction that my no-power relationship idea had inspired to the extent of dissolving a conventional marriage and starting a commune in her house, now went all the way. She gave her house to her eighteen-year-old daughter, quit her job as a judge, and went to live in the Virginia community. In giving away her worldly goods, she gave me her publishing company, which consisted of six xeroxed copies of my manuscript.

So there I was, the owner of a publishing company with only my own book to publish, by default, a self-publisher. My judge friend had given me a company name and the idea appealed to me. I took out a license, opened a bank account under the name Intergalactic Publishing Company, and drew up a logo. I typeset my book, did the layout and paste-up, learned about paper, printing, and distribution. Friends soon gathered around to help. The investment in money wasn't extreme, and besides I had faith in the book for the following reasons:

1. There are millions of people who need to pass exams and meet other challenges of life
2. The book tells, in detail, how to save time and energy in preparing for and passing exams
3. I know from my own experience that the method works
4. I had helped innumerable people learn self-hypnosis for all kinds of problems so I know it's useful for different kinds of people and problems.
5. There is published research on the usefulness of altered states of consciousness in everything from raising grades to lowering blood pressure

My faith seems to have been well placed. A stapled, manuscript-looking version sold, so I made a real book, typeset and properly bound with drawings and cover photos. Within a month my first printing of a thousand copies sold out, and before the second printing of three thousand was gone, Bill Whitehead, Senior Editor for E. P. Dutton, had discovered the book and offered to publish it.

I had already ordered a third printing of three thousand more and had grown into what seemed like a big company myself. Lots of friends were helping me, and we had moved into the Chateau, an apartment complex with a courtyard. Dealing with all the interpersonal problems of living together, while trying (sometimes unsuccessfully) to keep a no-power relationship business going, was taking most of my time and energy, and I didn't seem able to finish the next book I started. I decided to give my publishing company to my friends and sell my book to Dutton.

Now my friends are distributing the last three thousand copies, are selling another book we had helped an author self-publish, are helping more authors with self-publishing, and are doing other things I would never have thought of.

I am in my little hideaway being a writer again. I learned a lot about power relationships from owning my own business. Now I'm going to see if power relationships can be avoided while dealing with an "Establishment House." So far it looks very good. I am also eager to see how I respond to whatever fame and fortune ensues from this venture. It may be material for another book.

Freda Morris
2301 Stuart Street
Berkeley, Calif. 94705
January, 1975

SELF-HYPNOSIS IN TWO DAYS

CHAPTER ONE

Weekend Plan

Why Self-Hypnosis

You have to pass an exam; participate in a stringent interview or audition; overcome a set of obstacles to get a job, a license, a certificate, course credit, or a degree; or meet some other challenge. Whatever your reason you can lighten the burden of preparation, the strain of taking the test, and assure your success if you will spend two days learning how to use self-hypnosis as set forth in this book. There are people who are continually disappointed and those who arrange to get what they want and need. Which do you want to be?

In just three nights and two days you will learn a skill which will be valuable to you for the rest of your life. To get a high school diploma you spend six or eight hours a days, nine months of the year for twelve years.

A college degree takes four years. To develop competence in playing a musical instrument you may spend hours every day for many years. But to become proficient in hypnotizing yourself you need just one weekend from Friday afternoon to Monday morning.

Four simple steps are involved:

1. Read this book at least twice
2. Arrange an undisturbed weekend or its equivalent
3. Collect some easily available materials
4. Follow the step-by-step instructions

Definition

Self-hypnosis is a state of mind in which you have a unique control over your mental processes, your emotions, and your attitude. Self-hypnosis enables you to focus where you want to and to be calm, peaceful, concentrated, clearheaded, alert, totally engrossed in the mental activity of your choice, completely undistracted by outside interferences and irrelevant thoughts. Self-hypnosis has no known physical correlates and cannot be defined by any outside criteria, only your own subjective experience. In other words, it is as good as you believe it is.

Safety

Using self-hypnosis is as safe as going to sleep at night. It is a totally self-contained and self-controlled mental state which gives you self-determination rather than letting your fate be determined by chance or human frailty. With self-hypnosis you protect yourself from ever being hypnotized against your will or by chance.

When you have finished a self-hypnosis session you bring yourself out by counting backward from five to one. This returns you, rested and clearheaded, to ordinary consciousness.

The Setting

For success in self-hypnosis give yourself the most nearly ideal conditions possible. The most important is freedom from interruption. Rent a room and hang the "Do Not Disturb" sign on the door. Let only one person know where you are and instruct him to contact you only in extreme emergency. Or use a friend's apartment, put the phone in the refrigerator or in a box stuffed with pillows, and put a note on the door telling callers where your friend can be reached.

It is better to be in new surroundings so you won't be distracted by busywork around the house. But if you feel you must use your own quarters tell your family and friends that you are "taking a retreat" and will not be receiving calls or visitors until Monday.

Next, be sure the quarters you will occupy are suitable for the project. The room should be the most isolated in the house. Clear it of unfinished projects, books you've been wanting to read, radio, TV, or anything that might have a pull on your mind. Have easily prepared food available. Have a comfortable bed, chair, and a desk or writing table. Arrange easy access to a bathroom.

With your solitude assured you automatically turn your attention toward your inner experiences, thus facilitating learning hypnosis. You need not be concerned about becoming "shack happy" or feeling locked up during the weekend. The hypnotic trips you will be taking will be sufficiently fascinating to maintain your interest and enthusiasm.

Equipment

To your isolated room bring:

1. A pendulum, a locket, or any small weight on an eight-inch string
2. A candle and matches
3. A kitchen or photo timer
4. A tape recorder with remote switch and earphones
5. Two sixty-minute cassette tapes
6. Notebook and pen
7. Easily prepared food and nonalcoholic beverages

The pendulum enhances access to automatic muscle movements. The candle provides a fixation point. The timer alerts you at the end of sessions. The tape recorder is for recording and listening to descriptions of your experiences and instructions for going into hypnosis. The notebook helps in two ways. It increases your focus of attention on your experiences through the discipline of transcribing them onto paper, and the written record will be useful for future reference.

General Plan

Read through the entire book at least twice before starting the weekend program. During the weekend keep the book before you for constant referral. The time needed for the program is three nights and two full days in succession. However, if this is not possible for you, you can spread the program over several evenings. If you can spend six hours at a time you can expect to take about six evenings for the program.

For convenience we assume you begin early Friday evening and continue through until time to go to work Monday morning. Of course, it doesn't matter which days of the week you choose.

In the process of learning to go into a hypnotic state you will actually be acquiring skills which you will use to prepare for and pass all future exams or other challenges. You will avoid the struggle, wasted energy, self-recriminations, failures, and retrials that examination situations too often evoke. These difficulties result from trying to force yourself to prepare for and take the exam. With self-hypnosis you will learn a different kind of control over yourself which involves *allowing* rather than forcing yourself to do the things you need to do. As in Zen and karate, you go with the energy rather than opposing it and thus make use of it for your own ends.

You will learn how to use your imagination and self-suggestions to bring about muscle movements, sensations, emotions, and mental images. This will develop your ability to concentrate automatically, to recall effortlessly, to conceptualize clearly, and to apply your knowledge most effectively.

There are eight stages in the process of the weekend work. First, you will work with a pendulum for two purposes: To understand that your unconscious is a powerful force you can communicate with and use for your benefit, and to discover the kinds of problems you, personally, may be confronted with in learning hypnosis.

Second, you will learn to hypnotize yourself through eye fixation.

Third, you will learn to deepen your hypnotic state through hand levitation.

Fourth, you will begin hypnotic work on emotional control—learning to bring on a feeling, to set it aside or to change it.

Fifth, you will continue hypnotic work on attitude problems—discovering and changing harmful attitudes.

Sixth, you will learn to control mental activity—to remember to visualize, to organize, to conceptualize.

Seventh, you will apply hypnosis to studying for your exam or other challenge and make concrete plans for its continual use.

Eighth, you will start your daily program of hypnotizing yourself and making suggestions.

The two days are divided into three sections each; morning, afternoon, and evening, with an extra morning and evening. This gives eight divisions to the weekend into which the eight stages fit.

The following timetable is a guide through the weekend. Although it should not necessarily be rigidly adhered to, do not stray too far off schedule.

Timetable

Friday evening	Prehypnotic work with pendulum
Saturday morning	Induce hypnosis and learn how to come out of hypnosis
Saturday afternoon	Deepen hypnosis
Saturday evening	Develop emotional control
Sunday morning	Work on attitude problems
Sunday afternoon	Learn to control mental activity

Sunday evening	Plan for meeting challenges and applying hypnosis to study

Monday morning	Start daily program and return to normal activity

CHAPTER TWO

Prehypnotic Work

Let's assume that you have already read through the book twice and the dry runs are over. This is for real. You are in your isolated room, free from fear of interference; you have your equipment; and it is several hours before you will get sleepy. You are eager to see what you can learn right away.

At this point it is crucial to assume a patient attitude. However strong your desire to rush the preliminary exercises you should quell your impatience and take extra care to develop a sound foundation for your skill in self-hypnosis. Even though you have read the story before, read it again, and assiduously follow the instructions about taping and note taking. It is important that you get used to these routines before you get into later sections. Diligence in your work with the pendulum now will pay dividends when you start hypnosis proper.

Your pendulum can be made from a paper clip and piece of string or it can be a beautiful pendant on a gold chain. The important thing is the inherent quality of the pendulum to magnify the tiny inadvertent movements of your hand and arm.

Your unconscious is always answering questions but normally you are unable to receive this information. The pendulum makes it possible for you to ask "yes-no" questions and immediately get answers. A pre-arranged signal, such as its swing in a circle means "yes" and in a straight line means "no," must be set up. The following story serves as an illustration of how the pendulum can be used.

The Student and the Lost Bibliography

Susan was a twenty-seven-year-old graduate student who came to me frantic to find a single sheet of paper containing an important list of references.

"I've looked everywhere for that blasted piece of paper," Susan complained. "If I don't find it soon I just won't be able to get the project done. It would take me forever to find those references again. I just couldn't! Can hypnosis help me?"

I told her that we would first use the pendulum, which could reach her subconscious directly without the necessity for hypnosis. I explained that she would hold the chain of the pendulum in her fingers and that I would ask questions of her subconscious mind. If the pendulum swings in a circle it means "yes." If is goes in a straight line it means "no."

I got enough information from her to devise questions that were pertinent to the situation; then got her quieted down and holding the pendulum.

"Were you at school when you last saw the paper?" No.

"Were you at home when you last saw it?" Yes.

"Did you put it in with other papers?" No.

"Did you put it in an envelope by itself?" No.

"Did you put it in your purse?" No.

"Did you put it into some other container?" Yes.

"Did you put it in a bag?" Yes.

"Did you last see the paper at your desk?" No.

"Did you take it out of the room?" Yes.

"What in the world can that mean?" Susan asked. "I would have no reason to take it out of the room. I wouldn't use it anywhere else. And I had it right there with all the other crap for this project!" she added with rising annoyance.

"When were you working on it?" I asked for a second time.

"Like I told you, it was about a week ago that I *know* I was looking right at it. I have been working on other parts of the project since I lost it. I can't go any further without it."

"Let's go back to the pendulum and see what else we can learn," I suggested.

Through the pendulum we ascertained that she had last seen the bibliography on Monday, five days before.

"That's interesting," said Susan. "I wasn't working on the papers at all on Monday. I was putting together a large poster for part of my class presentation. I don't think I was even at my desk. I did most of the work on the kitchen floor. That doesn't make sense."

"Were you working with any kind of a bag on Monday?" I asked.

"No, I was working on the poster."

Back to the pendulum.

"Did you work with a bag on Monday?" Yes.

"Is the bag in the house now?" Yes.

"Is it in the room where your desk is?" No.

"Is it in the kitchen?" No.

"Is the bibliography in that bag?" Yes.

"Oh, I remember!" exclaimed Susan, dropping the pendulum. "I was using some things for the poster that I keep in a big bag: Tape, colored paper, rubber cement, and stuff like that. I put it back in the attic. Oh! And I remember using it on the desk just for a few minutes when my roomates came in and wanted to use the kitchen. I'll go home and see."

"Just a minute. Let's use the pendulum once more. Is the bibliography in the attic?" Yes.

Susan excitedly dashed away and soon called me.

"I found it. It was stuck to a big sheet of black construction paper with a drop of rubber cement. Now I remember putting the paper there to keep from getting glue on the desk. Somehow it got stuck to the bibliography.

"Thanks loads! Wow! What a relief!"

When you finish this paragraph turn on your recorder and set your timer for ten minutes, then lie down and close your eyes. Record your thoughts and feelings about the story and outline the questions it raises. Think about the story in terms of its importance to Susan. Imagine the tension, the excitement, the relief that came with the revelation through the pendulum. Think about its meaning and relevance for you, how you might use this technique for yourself.

What does it mean about the availability of your unconscious mind?

When your timer sounds listen to the recording and then turn it off and make clear, succinct notes of the experiences you had while reading the story and thinking about it. Note your attitude toward the task. Were you bored, impatient, interested, eager? Did you feel empathy for Susan? What would you want to find out? Are you eager to see if the pendulum will move in your hand? Are you worried that it won't? Are you feeling that this is a waste of time? Are you inclined to skip over it?

Your notes will be helpful in determining the nature of your hypnotic responsiveness, so don't take this task lightly.

When you have finished with your notes run your recorder back to the beginning. You won't need to listen to this recording again, and you are ready for taping whenever the occasion arises.

Before you use the pendulum yourself get up and do some vigorous exercise. Every hour or so throughout the weekend jump up and down for a few seconds, swing your arms wildly, or do something to get your heart pumping fast. This will keep you alert and prevent your going stale from the confinement.

The Pendulum Swings

Sit down at your table. Take a few moments to relax and assume this attitude: "The important thing is not

what happens but that I observe both what happens and my reaction to it."

Put your tape recorder and timer in a handy place where you can operate them with your free hand. Hold the chain or string of the pendulum between your thumb and forefinger so that the pendulum hangs about eight inches from your hand. With your elbow resting on the corner of the table fix your eyes passively on the pendulum.

Turn on your recorder and set your timer for two minutes. Now imagine the pendulum moving in a clockwise circle. Continually keep this image strongly in mind, while at the same time you speak your thoughts and feelings and your observations of the pendulum into your microphone.

When your timer sounds the end of two minutes listen to the recording (no need for the earphones yet) and make notes of the behavior of the ball and your own thoughts, feelings, and attitudes toward the task. Some typical examples of such notes follow:

"The ball moved in a clockwise direction almost immediately, and by the time the two minutes were up it was swinging in such a strong circle it almost pulled out of my grip. I was amazed and very pleased."

"The ball hung perfectly still for the two minutes, and my arm started aching. I kept my mind on the task but felt silly."

"Within thirty seconds the ball began to turn opposite to the way I was thinking. I was upset and feared that this might mean I am a stubborn or negative person. As soon as I was aware of my fear the ball stopped dead still and then moved in an erratic pattern for nearly a minute. I was confused and unable to concentrate."

What Type Are You?

Your two minutes with the pendulum are for diagnostic purposes; that is, to learn what your particular reaction pattern is to an attempt to control your unconscious muscle movements. Let's see what your pattern suggests about the kinds of problems you face in learning hypnosis.

One of three general patterns should predominate:

Type I: Strong, ready, and regular movement
Type II: Little or no movement
Type III: Erratic or contrary movement

No one of these patterns is more desirable than any other. The important thing is that you know which one you exhibit and how to use this knowledge to facilitate your success.

Type I—Easy come, easy go.

Prototype: Will Rogers, who deliberately made occasional mistakes with his rope twirling so his audience wouldn't get bored.

If you are a Type I the pendulum will have moved quickly and easily in a clockwise direction. You were probably eager to get on with the process and very happy with the outcome. If this is you, guard against a tendency to skip steps or hurry through the weekend program.

You probably have a natural talent for getting into deep hypnosis easily and can use hypnosis very effectively. Your flexibility and ease of inner psychic contact will be useless, however, unless, you train yourself carefully.

Talented people often fall short due to their failure

to prepare and the consequent discouragement at the ensuing difficulties. Refuse to allow your feelings of impatience to propel you to proceed without sufficient preparation. Only persistent, organized, structured effort will produce maximum accomplishment, so stick with the program step by step.

Type II—True Grit.

Prototype: Mattie Ross, a fourteen-year-old girl whose true grit led her to hunt down her father's killer against all odds.

If you are a Type II there will have been little or no movement of the pendulum. You probably have a critical, demanding attitude and a tendency to focus on external evidence of hypnotic accomplishment. Accept and note what you *are* able to experience. You can't force yourself to experience something, any more than you can deliberately be spontaneous. You must *allow* yourself to become aware of your experience. As a Type II, you, especially, must keep this in mind.

You have the important qualities of determination and persistence and need only relax. Turn the focus of your attention from the outward evidence of your success or failure to the nuances of feelings within. Give yourself lots of relaxation instructions and open yourself to soft, warm, good feelings. Use your imagination and do not demand fantastic changes in consciousness.

Lay your demanding attitude aside and see to it that you have a restful, relaxing weekend. If the quality of your performance on a task doesn't meet your high standards, simply accept it anyway and go on to the next step. Above all, don't fail to finish the program because you couldn't get some task completed to your satisfaction.

Type III—Don't tell *me* what to do.

Prototype: Dr. Fritz Perls, founder of Gestalt Therapy, whose last words were said to be, "Don't tell *me* what to do!"

If the pendulum exhibited an erratic or contrary pattern you are a Type III and can expect an unevenness of development of your hypnotic skills throughout the weekend. You will be able to follow some of the suggestions remarkably well but may have little feeling for other tasks. You may be inclined to handle this in one of two ways or perhaps both ways alternately.

One, you may spend an inordinate amount of time playing with the easy tasks and skip hurriedly over the hard ones.

Or, two, you may rush through the easy ones dismissing them as child's play and then struggle with the others until you finally declare them impossible.

Alerted to this state of affairs, keep your eye on the timetable. Remember that observation of yourself is the key and no one particular phenomenon is crucial. Be an interested observer of your emotional responses, both negative and positive. Often a negative response changes simply through your awareness.

Almost everyone will have difficulty setting aside a weekend and saying "No!" to all the interferences that arise. Once you find the time, tell all your friends right away that you will be busy then. Make a point of not even finding out about enticements such as special movies, plays, and so on. Once you have gone through the weekend program you will be able to get much more done in less time so the ultimate savings in time will be manyfold. Then you'll have more time to do these fun things.

If you are still unclear about your type you are probably a combination of two or even of all three. Nevertheless, you should be able to pick the one that predominates so you can give more weight to the warnings most appropriate for you. In all cases, be alert to obstacles that may interfere with your progress. Awareness is the key word.

Pendulum Play

The words *subconscious* and *unconscious* are sometimes used interchangeably in this book, but in general, *subconscious* refers to processes of the mind that can readily be brought into awareness or fairly easily controlled, while *unconscious* refers to processes that must, by their nature, be automatic. For example, you will be talking to your subconscious now in words and images. It will get the message and serve as a sort of mediator to the unconscious, which in turn will control the pendulum in the way described. One of the main values of playing with the pendulum is that you get a real gut-level feeling for the power that your fantasy can have over your unconscious.

To contact your subconscious mind you will employ five techniques:

1. Focusing on your breathing
2. Giving compelling instructions
3. Repeating them many times
4. Imagining a special magnetic force pulling the pendulum
5. Timing your words to your responses

You will suggest to the pendulum that it swing four different ways:

1. Clockwise

2. Counterclockwise
3. Back and forth (left and right)
4. To and fro (toward you and away)

Start by sitting down by your table with your
pendulum handy. Before you pick up the pendulum,
turn on the recorder and focus on your breathing for
about twenty deep breaths. Have the microphone close
enough to pick up the sounds of your breathing. Pay
minute attention to the air coming in, to the movement
of your chest and stomach, to the relaxation that comes
naturally.

Pick up the pendulum and hold it as before. Stare
at it and speak slowly, softly, yet distinctly and with
emphasis. You might begin, "I am staring deep into
the pendulum. I am becoming one with it. It is turning,
I am turning, we are turning, round and round."

If this sounds too mystical for your taste you might
begin, "I am imagining a spinning magnet, spinning in
a clockwise direction under the pendulum. It draws the
pendulum around, pulls it out and around, round and
round."

Find some patter (continuing verbalizations) that
appeals to you and go on and on with the suggestions.
Pick either of the above examples or make up something similiar. The important thing is that you keep
talking. As you speak the words imagine a special
magnet set up on a spinning arm under the pendulum
and drawing it around. After the pendulum has gone
in a clockwise direction, change the suggestion to
counterclockwise and continue on through the other

two directions. Time your suggestions to fit with your observations of the actual movement of the pendulum.

The ease of this task will vary widely among people. Some will go through the four different movements of the pendulum in less than five minutes. This speed is not necessarily advantageous. If the pendulum doesn't turn quickly for you, try each direction for at least five minutes. If it isn't swinging in the specified direction by then, give it some conscious help. Make such tiny movements that you are hardly sure that you are deliberately helping it. Don't think of this as cheating. Feeling the pendulum moving is good preparation for allowing it to turn by itself. In addition, seeing it turn gives you an actual observation to describe as you record. Remember that your purpose right now is to make a useful recording.

When you have finished the recording for all four movements of the pendulum, listen to the recording with your earphones while holding the pendulum and staring at it. You may find that it starts to swing before the suggestions begin, while you are still breathing along with your recorded breaths. If so, that is a good sign of your anticipating the suggestions to come. Listen all the way through, vividly imagining the moving magnet spinning around, pulling the pendulum.

If the pendulum doesn't move by itself within the five minutes, give it a little boost. Listen to the recording as many times as is necessary to get automatic movement. Continue until the pendulum's movements are clearly a result of the suggestions.

Spend the rest of the evening playing with the

pendulum. Make up some questions to ask it. You might ask about a lost article. You could try to remember to whom you loaned a certain book. "Was it a man? Was he over thirty? Was he married?" It's fun to recall a forgotten name. "Did it start with an A, a B, and so on? Was it an English name?"

Don't be disturbed by wrong or contradictory answers. The unconscious seems sometimes so eager to answer that it tries to give information it doesn't have or hasn't yet brought near enough to consciousness to share. Have fun!

CHAPTER THREE

Hypnotic Induction

"Do you know how to play the guitar?"

"Yes, I do. You hold it against your body with the strings facing away from you and the long part to the left. You press on the strings with the fingers of your left hand and move your right hand across the strings."

"Great! Would you play something for me?"

"I'm sorry, I don't play."

This is the situation you are in now with regard to hypnosis. You have read the book so you know how to hypnotize yourself, but you haven't got the skill of becoming hypnotized. Your purpose now is to develop this skill.

We will consider that you have fulfilled your purpose when you can bring about the following conditions with your hypnotic induction procedure:

1. You can induce a sensation in your eyelids
2. They will automatically shut on signal
3. You are unable to open them with effort

This first condition can be either a feeling of heaviness, a stinging and burning sensation, or a rapid blinking and fluttering. Your eyelids will decide for you which they will use. Any of the three is equally useful in bringing about eyelid closure.

Self-hypnosis was defined earlier as a state of mind in which you have a unique control over yourself. This control is unique in that it is an allowing rather than a forcing kind of relationship with yourself. So the second thing you do is to develop automatic response in a small muscle group. Rather than forcing your eyes shut, you allow them to close. The eyelid is chosen because its small size makes it easy to condition or train; tiredness is quickly induced through staring; and closing of the eyes cuts out vision, thus aiding hypnotic induction.

The third condition, having the eyes stick shut, is called eyelid catalepsy. It is an interesting experience, exciting to accomplish, and helpful in maintaining the hypnotic state.

The purpose of inducing catalepsy is that the idea of allowing rather than forcing is brought home very strongly by this experience. You can't force your eyes open but they open easily when you allow them to. You will learn more about this by experience. But before we go on to induce hypnosis through eye fixation and subsequent eyelid catalepsy, let's see about coming out of hypnosis.

How to Come Out of Hypnosis

When you hypnotize yourself you will not feel any great and dramatic change in consciousness. You will still know who you are, where you are, when it is and what you have to do later. If you want to you can be an excellent judge of how long you've been hypnotized.

When you are ready to return to ordinary waking consciousness, you simply say to yourself (aloud or silently) that you will come back alert and wide awake, rested, and feeling fine. Then you count backward slowly, and at the count of "one" your eyes open and you are in ordinary consciousness. If you are very deep and very relaxed, you may want to count back from ten or twenty just to give yourself time to reorient pleasantly. If you are in a fairly light state, you will find that counting from five to one is sufficient.

How to Go into Hypnosis

You will use eye fixation to begin the hypnotic induction procedure and will condition or train your eyelids in the following manner:

At the signal

"one" your eyelids get heavy or sting or flutter

"two" your eyes close

"three" they lock shut

Remember that getting the eyes quickly closed is not the point of this procedure. The important thing is that you experience the *sensation*, feel your eyelids operating *independently* of your conscious control, and that you actually *lose the ability* to open your eyes. *And* that all this occurs on *signal*.

The first step is to study your particular reactions to suggestions of eyelid heaviness and then to use your discoveries to design the first part of a personalized hypnotic induction procedure. The reason we choose to focus on heaviness as opposed to stinging or fluttering is that it is most commonly encountered and is convenient to deal with. You aren't necessarily expected to feel heaviness. Don't worry if you don't. The purpose of this exercise is to determine what you *do* experience.

Place your candle and tape recorder on your table, light the candle, and seat yourself comfortably in front of it. Shut your eyes and take twenty slow, deep breaths, exhaling completely. Now open your eyes and center your attention on the candle. Allow everything else to go out of focus or even vanish if it will.

Assume a dreamy attitude toward the candle. Wonder about the flame, what it is, and why it is hot. Think about the wax and the humming bees that made it. Let the thoughts filter through your consciousness. Don't actively bring them on.

If you feel distracted by something, deliberately convert the distraction (sight, sound, or thought) into a force that will contribute toward your hypnotic induction instead of detracting from it. For example, if a light bothers you, tell yourself silently that the light streaming toward you is pushing you into relaxation. If you hear automobiles going by, tell yourself that the sounds are bringing you deeper into awareness of the candle. If an annoying thought pesters you, tell yourself that every time it comes into your mind the candle glows more brightly.

After two or three minutes of following your associations about the candle, turn your attention to your eyelids. Become aware of their weight while continuing to stare at the candle flame. Remind yourself that they do weigh something and that effort is required to keep them open.

Focus on a feeling of heaviness for five minutes or so. Precise timing is not essential, and it is better not to bother with the timer at this point.

Enhance the feeling of heaviness by saying aloud, slowly but firmly, "One, your eyelids are getting heavy, very heavy. Heav—y, heav—y."

Repeat this suggestion over and over for a minute or so. Then pause while strongly focusing on heaviness. Alternate silent focusing and verbal suggestions. If your eyes close by themselves, quickly say "two" aloud just as they close. You don't want to miss a single opportunity to associate their closing with the signal "two." If they have not closed after five minutes, slowly and gently close them, saying "two" as you do so.

Now turn on your recorder and describe in as much detail as possible exactly what your sensations and feelings were during this experience. Include the early part when you were taking deep breaths, and also the time when you were gazing at the candle passively. Especially emphasize the sensations in your eyes after you began giving the heaviness suggestions. Did your eyes feel heavy? Did they sting or burn? Did they blink rapidly and flutter shut?

Listen to the recording and make careful notes. Your job now is to develop the part of the hypnotic patter which works best to bring about automatic eyelid closure. The trick in developing an effective patter is to make use of your particular reactions to eye fixation and heaviness instruction.

For instance, did your eyes feel heavy? Then focus on heaviness something like this:

"As your eyelids continue to get heavier and heavier enhance that feeling of heaviness by imagining that they are made of lead and are so very heavy that they have to close down. One. Little lead weights are tied to your eyelashes pulling them down very, very heavy. The little muscles are sooo relaxed they just can't lift anymore. Two. They close down."

Did your eyes sting and burn? Then:

"As you continue to stare at the candle, notice the sensation in your eyes. They get tired, very tired. They begin to sting and burn. One. They are stinging worse and worse, so badly that all you can think about is how

wonderful it will feel to have them shut. The stinging and burning makes them want to close sooo badly. Sooo badly! They are shutting, closing down, two, shut, all the way shut. It feels so good to have them closed."

Did your eyes blink more and more rapidly? Then:

"Notice how your eyes are starting to blink more and more often. The rate is increasing more and more. One. They are blinking so fast that you can hardly see. They are fluttering closed but they are barely opening back up. They are closing. Two. They are closing all the way."

The samples are stated in the second person because this gives a feeling of distance and objectivity. It is different from your usual way of referring to yourself as "I," thus it is more apt to hold your attention.

Study the ideas you have put in your notes and think about ways you need to modify these sample hypnosis induction procedures. Use your own observations of yourself to change them to fit your particular needs.

Remember to make use of the techniques you learned when you were working with the pendulum:

1. Deep breathing
2. Compelling instructions
3. Repetition
4. Imaginative imagery
5. Timing your responsiveness

When you have carefully designed an induction patter, write it out and record it, reading it slowly with pauses and emphasis. (If you have eyelid flutter, you might speak quickly when referring to the flutter to capture the feeling of rapidity.) You may want to begin with an introduction something like this:

"Look deep into the center of the candle. As you do so breathe slowly and deeply, exhaling completely. As you exhale feel the relaxation that naturally comes across your chest when you breathe out. Let that relaxation spread over your body."

Even though it is unnecessary at this point, count back from five to one at the end of the taping. It is always better to count yourself out after even part of an induction procedure. For one thing, it gets you into the habit of coming out the way you ultimately want to, that is, by counting. Secondly, it is a safety precaution. You may have successfully hypnotized yourself and not realize it, so it's better to count yourself back.

Listen to the tape several times, following the instructions as best you can. Between sessions make notes of new observations, modify your procedure, and note the effect of the changes. Perfect the patter and listen to it over and over until your eyes develop their sensation and close on signal every time. When you are confident that you have succeeded with these two steps you are ready to study your reaction to eyelid catalepsy suggestions.

It is necessary to do this with three different kinds of suggestions in order to find out which works best for you. To do this you will go through your eye fixation and closure procedure by talking aloud three times, and each time including a different catalepsy suggestion. Don't worry about the exact wording. Just repeat all the general ideas using the same tone and manner as on the tape.

At the point where your eyes close, instead of counting yourself back out as the tape did, add a catalepsy suggestion. The three are presented below in the order in which you should use them. They are condensed, and you should expand and reiterate them so that your overall hypnotic induction is at least a minute longer than it was before. After you finish each induction procedure, count yourself back and make notes of your reaction to the catalepsy suggestions.

1. Catalepsy suggestion: immobility.

"The little muscles of your eyelids have completely gone to sleep. They are sooo relaxed they cannot possibly make another move. They are totally immobile. Three. Your eyes cannot be opened until those muscles are awakened. Even if you try hard they don't open. There is no way to force them open."

2. Catalepsy suggestion: glued.

"Feel the edges of your lids touching together. As they touch together they stick to each other. Three.

There is a special kind of glue on the edges that is drying quickly and sealing them tight. You cannot open them no matter how you try."

3. Catalepsy suggestion: sewed.

"Your eyes are closed shut now. You can't open them. Three. They are being sewed together by a team of little tailors. Stitched together. They are putting little padlocks on your eyes. You can't get them open no matter how hard you try."

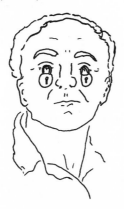

When you have finished making notes on the third trial put some fresh tape in your recorder and talk about your reactions. Be sure you have touched on everything you could possibly notice about the experiences. You are about to design the final part of your induction tape and you need all the information about yourself you can get. Listen to your recordings and compare yourself to the following summaries of three different reactions:

First person,

"My eyes feel very heavy when I'm hypnotizing myself and sort of clunk shut like the door of a vault, so I expected to respond best to the immobility suggestions. Actually I had a good feeling about all the suggestions. The first time my eyes felt totally immobile. The second time I could feel an overwhelming stickiness. The third time I could imagine the sewing very vividly and I even heard the click of the padlocks.

"I still think I could open my eyes if I tried but I believe I will learn not to be able to. I am going to incorporate all the styles into my hypnotic induction."

Second person,

"I responded just so-so to the immobility and sewed suggestions. I couldn't get into them very much but I really liked the glue.

"My eyes had been burning terribly. I imagined the glue was cool and soothing. I could feel it taking away all the burning while sticking my eyes together so they wouldn't open and burn any more. I'm going to use this one in finishing my induction tape. I'm sure I won't be able to open my eyes."

Third person,

"My eyelids had been blinking very fast so the idea that the little muscles of my eyelids had gone to sleep was ridiculous. They were actually going wild and practically in spasm. The heaviness suggestions about immobility didn't do a thing for me.

"I hated the idea of glue on the edges of my lids. My eyes opened again after they had closed that time and I could feel the stringy, rubbery glue pulling loose and popping from upper to lower lids. It was terrible and I counted myself out as fast as I could.

"I liked the little tailors best. I could almost feel the needles quickly sewing my lids shut but it didn't hurt. In fact, it was a relief because then I knew my eyes would stay shut. They continued to sort of flutter but didn't open any more."

Now, just as you designed a hypnotic patter that led to your success in the first two steps of getting into a hypnotic state, you must design the last part of the patter so as to bring about eyelid catalepsy.

Use what you know about yourself and what you know about the principles of effective suggestions. Write out what you want to say and tape it onto the other patter. Record over the counting back that you have at the end of the first patter. Once you have it done listen to it again and again. Make notes of new observations and improve and perfect the patter as you did before.

After you have perfected the tape and hypnotized yourself with it several times, turn off the recorder and hypnotize yourself by talking aloud. Don't strive for exact wording but do follow the general design you have developed. Next, hypnotize yourself by going through the whole procedure silently. Do all three several times: the tape, aloud, and silently. See which works best but develop skill with them all.

By now you may be feeling confident that you won't be able to get your eyes open if you try. Whether you will succeed with eye catalepsy or not, it is time to test yourself. (Remember that success here is allowing yourself to *fail* to get your eyes open.)

When testing the strength of your eyelid catalepsy it is important not to actually get your eyes open. When you are ready for the test, hypnotize yourself aloud or silently. Then do the following:

Put your finger on the top of your head and try to look at it through your skull. That is, roll your eyes back into your head as far as possible while they are shut. Continue concentrating on your finger and the spot it is touching, at the same time telling yourself that you can't open your lids.

When you are concentrating well, gingerly and very gently try to open your eyes. Your eyebrows should lift but your lids should stay closed. Don't try too long. If you feel them starting to open stop immediately and continue practicing.

Repeat this test often until you are convinced that your eyes are really cataleptic. After several successful tests try it without your finger on top of your head.

It is quite a thrill when you can really do your best to open your eyes and they just won't open. When this happens to you you *know* you are in a different state of consciousness. You have learned to shunt the nerve impulses in your brain away from the place they normally go when you try to open your eyes. It is a matter of simply learning *not* to use the right muscles.

Unless you got a very early start this morning it may be well past noon. If it is approaching two or three o'clock you should move on to the next section even if you have some doubt about how completely cataleptic your eyelids are. If you have the first two signs of hypnosis working well, then the catalepsy will come along as you learn deepening in the next chapter.

CHAPTER FOUR

Hypnotic Deepening

Let's hope that you remembered to exercise every hour or so through the morning. If you did forget occasionally, you need give the question no further concern, for now you know how to hypnotize yourself and can use hypnotic suggestion to assure that you will remember.

The next time you are in a hypnotic state simply say, "Approximately every hour, at a convenient time, you will remember to exercise vigorously. You will take the kind of exercise that will benefit you most and will enjoy it very much."

Now that you can hypnotize yourself, there is another thing you should do right away. Early in the discussion of the value of hypnosis I pointed out that you can use self-hypnosis to avoid going into a hypnotic state inadvertently. When hypnotized tell yourself, "You can hypnotize yourself easily and well and you can allow yourself to be hypnotized by a person of your choice whenever you want to. But you will *never* go into a hypnotic state inadvertently in a dangerous situation such as when driving. And you will never allow yourself to be hypnotized by anyone whom you don't trust." Repeat this to yourself some time when you are in a hypnotic state.

In the hypnotic deepening you will use your imagination to bring about hand levitation, the automatic floating of your hand. The imagination is a very powerful tool. It has been depreciated in our culture and is often used in the phrase, "*just* the imagination," implying that it is of no consequence. Nothing could be more wrong. The imagination is the prime force initiating everything we accomplish. "Imagination" is from the same Latin root as "image." We image or visualize something before we actualize it.

This suggests that imagination is limited to visual imaging, but you can also imagine the smell of a rose, the sensation of riding on a merry-go-round, the coolness of a linoleum floor as you step on it with bare feet. Another quality of the imagination is that it has a direct line of communication to the subconscious and, hence, to the unconscious. You are going to make use of this fact in a few minutes to induce hand levitation and thereby deepen your hypnotic state.

Hand levitation is a strange and wonderful feeling that can *only* come about through your imagination. There is no way to force, demand, or command this experience. Millions of times you have wanted to raise your hand and you have done so through the force of your will. If you simply wanted your hand raised into the air you would again force it into the desired position. But the purpose of this exercise is to give you the experience of feeling the effects of your imagination in controlling sensations to such a striking degree that an autonomous movement results.

When you are ready, make sure that your hands and arms are free and separated from each other. They should be resting on your thighs with no table or anything above them that your hand will bump into as it rises.

Hypnotize yourself silently. After you are hypnotized and resting comfortably in your chair with your eyes stuck shut, become aware of the attention focused on your eyes. Think of your attention as something that flows from one thing to another under your direction. Indeed it is, but we don't always take charge of our attention or take responsibility for where it goes. In the hypnotic state you can make your attention really your own.

Imagine your attention flowing down the right side of your neck as it leaves your eyes. Become hyperaware of the muscles of your neck and shoulder as your attention moves. Notice that the muscles relax even more as you pass by them with your mind tuned into them.

Feel your attention move on down your arm and into your hand. Slowly become more and more aware of everything about your hand. Gradually, one after the other, tune into such qualities as the texture that it is touching, its position, its shape and size, its temperature, its weight. As you focus more and more intently to the

exclusion of all else, you may be able to detect a difference between the temperature of the palm and that of
the back of your hand.

Imagine as vividly as possible the movement of the
blood through your hand. It really is moving all the
time and you can feel it by concentrating closely
enough. Look for a throbbing and a tingling in your
fingertips. Continue this exercise in hand awareness for
five minutes or so, then bring yourself out of the hypnotic state by counting backward as usual.

Now make careful notes of every experience you can
remember. Did you follow your attention down your
face, neck, and arm? Did the muscles relax as your
attention passed by? Did you feel a throbbing, tingling,
or pulsing sensation? Could you feel the texture your
hand was touching? List all the sensations of which you
were aware. Tell how each felt. As you may suspect, you
are analyzing the particular responsiveness of your hand
in preparation for developing a deepening patter.

Now set up your tape recorder with fresh tape,
hypnotize yourself, and after you are hypnotized, without opening your eyes or disturbing your state, turn on
your recorder. Talking in a quiet voice at a slow pace,
carefully review in detail all the things you said silently
the last time you hypnotized yourself, adding any new
sensations you experience. Tell yourself that your body
is relaxed, your eyes are locked shut, and call attention
to the various sensations in your hand.

You might say:

"Your attention is moving from your eyes down your
cheek to your jaws. Feel the bundle of jaw muscles

relax. As they let go your mouth opens slightly. Now your attention is moving through your neck. As your neck relaxes, your head sinks down very comfortably. Your attention is crossing over toward your right shoulder. As it passes across your throat, you feel your voice box relax. Hear the change in the sound. Your shoulder totally relaxes and your attention moves down your arm, and so on."

As you continue, speak slowly and with emphasis, commenting on what you are experiencing. Especially note increases in the intensity of any sensation. The idea is to become aware of changes more and more quickly and to direct those changes by directing your attention and using the power of your imagination. For example, awareness of blood flow within your fingers often leads to a tingling sensation. Comment on this by saying, "You feel a tingling sensation growing stronger and stronger." Stating it in this way has the effect of causing it to become clearer.

You may detect air currents, the dampness of your hand, itching, or other sensations. As they come into awareness comment on them in the same way. Awareness leads to control. You are working directly toward control of the feeling of the weight of your arm.

To this end imagine that your arm is made of lead. Visualize the color, the texture, the heaviness of lead. Describe it into your recorder. As you relax your arm more and more, point out the relaxation to yourself. When you feel the heaviness, emphasize it. After you have felt a definite response, change the image from heaviness to one of lightness. Imagine your hand and arm made of light, fluffy styrofoam. Visualize balloons attached to your wrist, filled with gas and pulling, lifting up, lighter and lighter.

Use your breathing to bring lightness into your arm. For example, you might say, "With each breath you take, the balloon is getting bigger and is pulling harder." Or, "Your arm is a balloon and each breath is blowing it up, lighter and lighter."

Now bring yourself out of hypnosis and listen to your tape without going back into hypnosis. Make notes about your experience and pick out the important aspects. Do you feel tingling easily? Can you feel your pulse by just concentrating on it? Did you respond easily to heaviness and lightness suggestions? Did the image of lead and styrofoam help? Did the balloons help?

Now hypnotize yourself again without using the recorder, and after you achieve eyelid catalepsy give suggestions designed to bring on lightness in your hand and arm. Continue until you feel the sensation clearly. It may take only a few minutes or it may take hours. Do not continue any one session to the point of weariness. If you get weary take a break and begin again.

When you stop and start over you are not wasting time. You will be increasing your hypnotic skill and will be taking steps toward hand levitation even though you may not be aware of your progress right away.

Eventually you will feel lightness, clearly and unquestionably. When you do, reach over with your left hand and pull up on your right wrist very, very gently.

Say to yourself, "An additional balloon is tied to your wrist and is pulling it up into the air."

Imagine the balloons as vividly as you can—the color, the shape, the size. Continue pulling upward until your right hand is no longer touching your thigh. If your arm is very easy to lift, gradually release it and see if it will continue to float by itself. Keep the floating suggestions going all the time. Whether you are talking silently or aloud speak slowly, firmly, clearly, and with emphasis.

If your arm does not stay up by itself continue to hold it and begin a patter focused around the idea of shunting the nerve impulses from the muscles in your arm to a new place in your brain where they won't be registered. That is, send the information from your arm to some place in your brain that can't make use of it. You want your brain to be in the dark about what your arm muscles are doing. You might say something like this:

"The connections from your arm muscles to your brain are turning off, are being shunted over to some other part of your brain where they make no impression. You just can't get any feedback from those muscles. They can lift your arm up and you won't know it. It will feel as if it is being pulled up by the balloons. Go ahead, hold it there. You won't feel any effort. Gently, slowly. It is floating.''

At the point where you say, "Go ahead, hold it there," actually bring just enough tension into your arm to support it. Let go with your left hand. Ignore the sensations of muscle tension as much as possible. With experience you will be able to cut out the sensations completely. Practice over and over until it actually does float.

Imagine breezes blowing it around and feel it respond to the breezes. Imagine a breeze blowing it toward your face and let it float over until it touches your face. You will be very excited and pleased when you feel it. It *is* delightful!

Let your hand float to your face. If it doesn't float in a reasonable length of time help it with muscular effort but act "as if" it is floating. Let the touch on your face be a signal for your hand to fall limply into your lap. Suggest that when this happens your whole body relaxes totally and you go deeper into a hypnotic state. Bring yourself out when you are ready.

By now you know enough about your own reactions to the various instructions to add a good deepening patter to your hypnotic induction tape. Keep in mind that as you become more experienced in hypnotizing yourself you will respond more quickly, so be prepared to revise your tape whenever you need to.

This time, instead of writing out your instructions and reading them into the recorder, record them directly from your experience as you give yourself the hand levitation suggestions. Find the place on your induction tape where you count yourself out and set the recorder to record over the counting. Before you turn it on, however, go through an induction procedure and bring yourself into a hypnotic state. Then, without opening your eyes or arousing yourself, turn on the recorder and record your deepening patter while at the same time responding to it.

After your hand has floated to your face and dropped into your lap, spend five or ten minutes very leisurely suggesting the most pleasant, relaxing images you can think of. Or, if you prefer, simply say, "Sleep," every ten or fifteen seconds for five or ten minutes. You will almost certainly feel the effects of deepening.

You will feel the deepening of the state in many different ways. Your body will relax more completely and you will feel yourself sink deeper into your chair or bed. You will have a feeling of withdrawing your interest from your surroundings. A sensation of blissfulness may overcome you. Whatever you feel, enhance it with suggestions which describe and amplify it.

Continue this process for a few minutes and then return your attention to your hand. Again go through the sequence of suggestions which cause your hand to float. Notice that you are more effective this time—that it floats more easily and quickly than before. The complete autonomy of the hand movement will be more profound. After your hand is back at rest, enjoy total relaxation for a few minutes. Take this opportunity to give yourself some suggestions that will contribute to the effectiveness and enjoyment of the weekend.

"I am very pleased; indeed, I am delighted with my progress. I am really getting into the swing of the weekend. I will continue to learn very quickly. I can hardly wait to get into the work with emotions. I'm filled with enthusiasm! I've never been so enthusiastic in my life before! I'm coming back now, alert, wide awake, and eager to continue this wonderful adventure. Five, four, three, two, one!"

Notice that this particular suggestion is not phrased in the second person. When you are talking about something very personal or are expressing the emotion you are inducing, it is sometimes better to speak in the first person.

You now have the basic skills for hypnotic work and have just started to use them to your advantage. You know that you can communicate with your unconscious. You can induce sensations in both small and large areas (eye and hand) and bring about autonomous movement in both muscle groups. You can develop catalepsy and levitation and you have probably experienced several other useful phenomena such as relaxation, dissociation, and vivid imagery. Now you are ready to learn to do hypnotic work.

CHAPTER FIVE

Hypnotic Work:
Emotional Control

Hypnotic work is presented under three headings in the next three chapters; emotional control, attitude control, and mental control. These aren't perfectly separable, so each shades into the other. For instance, your emotions will depend to some extent on your attitudes. Getting in touch with and changing your emotions uses vivid recall, which is a mental function. When you have worked your way through all three chapters, you will have a good grasp on how to do hypnotic work and will be ready to learn to apply it to exams or any challenge.

If your emotions get in the way when intellectual prowess is needed, you *must* develop emotional control to prepare for and pass any intellectual task. Do not fear that developing emotional control will make you an unfeeling person. On the contrary, emotional control allows you to be *more* in touch with your feelings as well as to set them aside when they are interfering with what you are doing. Emotional control gives you options as to when to deal with your feelings and gives you methods for dealing with them.

The emotional control chapter covers inducing or bringing on an emotion, coming out of or setting aside an emotion, and applying emotional control. By learning how to deal with your emotions at leisure, you can certainly have them better in hand when difficult situations arise.

Don't get hung up on how pure your emotions are, that is, whether you are *really* experiencing this emotion or that or something else entirely. The semantics of emotions is difficult. The important thing is that you use hypnosis to become aware of *some* kind of feelings and change them.

Emotions will inevitably be mixed up with sensations, body stances (such as clenching your teeth), memories, desires, and expectations. Accept all this and don't hassle yourself trying to separate them all out. Refuse to let confusion or lack of clarity stand in your way. Go right ahead doing the best you can.

The emotions that most commonly interfere with study and exam success are fear and anxiety, resentment and restlessness, and boredom and apathy. Fear and anxiety more often interfere with performance, whereas resentment and restlessness and boredom and apathy are more apt to interfere with preparation.

There may be other emotions that you experience

as interfering with your success. The techniques you learn here can be used to discover and deal with them whatever they are.

Inducing an Emotion

Though it is often advisable to talk to yourself in hypnosis as if you are talking to someone else, when working with emotions you will find that referring to yourself as "I" in some of your hypnotic suggestions is desirable. It seems that the intensity of the emotional state is heightened by the intimacy of the personal pronoun. Examples and your own experience will guide you.

Ways to manipulate an emotion:

1. Imagine a situation to bring it on
2. Remember an event that evoked it in the past
3. Act *as if* you are feeling it
4. Give yourself direct suggestion to enhance it

Turn your attention inward right now. Let your mind move about over your concerns. What one word could best describe the emotional state you are developing now as you focus on your possible emotions. Are you happy? Enthusiastic? Excited? Worried? Doubtful? Angry? Bored? Anxious? Regretful? What?

You will probably find that as you think on each emotion some of them seem to come over you just from your considering them. It might be that, "I wasn't worried at all. I had my mind on the weekend's work but now that you mention it there is such and such that worries me."

Or, "I wasn't thinking about it and hadn't in days but I am regretful that I did such and such."

Or, "I wasn't bored at the moment but, in general, with my job and all—"

This is evidence of control. You have brought on these feelings by shifting your attention. And obviously you had kept the feelings away by not attending to them.

You will find that some of the feelings or emotions (we use the words more or less interchangeably) don't apply to you now. Some of the others are more pertinent.

Next you will hypnotize yourself to bring out one of the feelings more clearly and increase its intensity. After that you will decrease its intensity and remove the feeling entirely.

To do this well you will need to give special attention to getting into a hypnotic state of some depth. Hypnotize yourself and deepen the state by inducing hand levitation several times. That is, get your hand to float, let it fall into your lap after it touches your face, and then get it to float up again. Continue deepening until you feel very removed from your ordinary mental state. Even though you are still fully aware of who you are, where you are, and that you are hypnotizing yourself, your mind can still become very quiet and focused. When this happens, time will seem to move very slowly in a most delicious way. Outside noises may disappear. Even if they don't they will not bother you.

When you are feeling quite removed from ordinary consciousness, say something like the following to yourself, recording what you say:

"Whatever emotion is nearest to your awareness, whatever is most readily available to you, will come clearer and clearer into your awareness. You are becoming more and more acutely aware of your inner sensations and feelings. You are letting images float through your mind that are clearly evoking the emotion in you. Now it is growing strong and vivid. You are (fill in with the correct emotion)."

You must, of course, modify the suggestions to fit your experience. No doubt you will need to take much more time than the brief paragraph above suggests.

Focus on the emotion that you have detected once it comes clearly to you. Build it up by making specific suggestions about it. Describe the sensations and images that accompany it. For example: "My anger is growing stronger. I feel my heart beating faster; my jaw muscles are tensing; my face is getting warm. I am recalling vividly how that son-of-a-bitch did me in." Describe in great detail everything you can think of that will increase the intensity of your feeling.

Go through this process with emotions that are pleasant and unpleasant, positive and negative. Whatever it is, work with it hypnotically as suggested above until you bring it to a peak. Continue suggestions for increasing the intensity until you find that it will not grow any stronger.

Emotions need not be avoided or overcontrolled. No matter how angry you get, you don't have to hurt anyone. No matter how sad you get, you don't have to kill yourself. No matter how happy and excited you get, you don't have to impose your trip on others.

Coming Out of an Emotion

Once you have increased the emotional state to its peak, give hypnotic suggestions to decrease it. When you are at the peak, there is nowhere to go but down. *Allow* the emotion to disappear. Your expectation that it will leave may be sufficient to cause it to go. Use hypnotic techniques, as outlined below, to increase the speed and efficiency of the change. The methods you use will have to be individualized depending on the emotion and its roots.

For example, if your feeling is sadness over some event that was very important to you, you may need to cry before it can truly diminish. Tell yourself that it is all right to cry; indeed, that it is desirable to let the tears roll. While you are crying give suggestions that the tears are washing away all the leftover feelings and leaving you clean and free. Then as it diminishes, suggest that you have it all cried out and are coming back feeling good.

If you are excited about the prospect of some coming event, you can diminish that feeling easily by a direct approach. Just tell yourself that the feeling is leaving and focus on the signs of its diminishing. "My heart rate is slowing down. My image of (the coming event) is fading." Then turn your mind strongly to something else.

If you are angry over some injustice or slight, you may need to use creative fantasy to dissipate the intensity of the anger in order to get good control over it. Imagine getting the best of the person who is the object of your anger. Picture it all in detailed images. If it is a verbal battle, you say all the clever things. If it is a physical fight, you hit all the good blows. Don't hold yourself back.

If you were raised with the mistaken idea that a hostile *thought* is as evil as a hostile *act,* give the question some serious consideration before you begin inducing emotions. Such an idea leads to guilt feelings over fantasies and thus eliminates one of the best and safest methods of handling anger.

The power of a clear image held in the mind and the strength of this image to change reality is one of the important points of this book. However, this is entirely different from using fantasy to free yourself from charged emotions. It is important to differentiate between wishing someone was actually dead or hurt and using a fantasy of killing or hurting him for your own emotional release.

Go ahead and fantasize to the limit of your ability and desire. Let it all out, then forget it. The person about whom you had the fantasy is now free of the negative thoughts that would be issuing from your subconscious mind and you are free from the suppressed feelings.

Awareness of your emotions is vital in dealing with them. Use your recorder. Listen back and make notes. Be creative in designing better ways to induce and remove emotions.

Applying Emotional Control

The amount of time you spend dealing with your more complex emotions and those which are more difficult to dissipate will depend on whether you anticipate problems with them in passing your exams. Don't let your focus be swayed from the ultimate goal. Don't, for example, let yourself become so fascinated with your emotions that you forget to work toward exam passing.

Let's move on to emotions most likely to need attention. One thing is almost certain, that exams, or any situation reminiscent of them, make you fearful and anxious. You certainly want to change that. Practically everyone feels some anxiety when facing an exam and it always hampers performance. Do not be misled by those who tell you anxiety is desirable, that it keeps you awake, gives you energy, and motivates you. Actually, it wastes energy and makes you try so hard that you can't allow the flow of your thoughts to lead you to the right answers. Anxiety is bad during exams! Calmness may feel strange at such times but so will your high scores.

To get a handle on examination anxiety take yourself into a fairly deep hypnotic state and recall a specific exam in which you were particularly anxious. In the hypnotic state memories quickly become vivid. As your memory becomes more and more vivid, encourage it by focusing on the details of the experience. Note carefully what you remember. Who sat next to you? What were they wearing? What were you wearing? Note initials carved on the desk, the voice of the examiner, the odor of someone's cigarette.

The process of exploring this memory will take you deeper into the hypnotic state and hence will increase your ability to remember. All the time you will become less and less aware of your body, your surroundings, the time and circumstances. You will feel more and more as if you really are in the exam room taking that exam. You may even begin to remember the questions asked and the answers that you gave.

Continue with this exercise until you can no longer detect an increase in sharpness and clarity, that is, until the memory stabilizes.

At this point turn your attention to your anxiety during the exam. As the feelings become more vivid, see if you can detect them in your body. Keep a strong image of the exam room in your mind, seeing it from the perspective of the place you sat during the exam. Pay attention to your body sensations as you imagine the scene in which you took the exam.

Now focus on the anxiety you felt during the exam. Through hypnotic suggestions, increase the anxiety and clarify its components. Are your hands sweaty? Is your mouth dry? Do you have butterflies in your stomach?

Are your shoulders tight? Is your mind all ascatter? Explore the details until you can find nothing more that is new.

Then, one by one, suggest all the symptoms away. Spend as much time as necessary. Use what you learned in the previous sections. When all your anxiety is gone, imagine you are very calmly taking the exam. Bring yourself out of the hypnotic state feeling fine.

Make thorough notes of your experience. Compare it with your memory of the way you actually felt during the exam. Study your notes for ideas about ways to induce, reduce, and otherwise modify your emotional state through hypnotic techniques.

Outline a hypnotic patter that will be most helpful for getting you into the feeling of examination anxiety and one which will get you out. Now hypnotize yourself again and induce and remove anxiety several times. When you feel really satisfied with your ability to do this bring yourself to the ordinary state of consciousness, feeling good.

After a break, go through a similar process with the feeling of resentment. You might use the image of a situation in which you had to do some meaningless homework that interfered with your attending a favorite play. Either use an incident you can remember or make one up. After developing the feeling of resentment, imagine trying to study and watch for signs of restlessness.

Do the same thing with boredom, perhaps using a dull lecture to induce it. Note the associated apathy as you imagine trying to write a term paper on one of the lecture topics that is of little interest. In each case, thoroughly dispel the destructive emotion and replace it with one that facilitates your accomplishing the task: active acceptance, steady concentration, interest, energetic enthusiasm.

If you have located any special emotional problems other than these that are causing you trouble, work on them in the same way.

When you are all through and ready to go on to attitudes, spend a few minutes thinking about the distinctions between the experience of manipulating your emotions this way and forcing yourself to do something you don't want to do. Notice that you can't force the emotions to change in any way. Coercion plays no role whatsoever. The way you *can* control the emotions is by becoming aware of them, using images, memories, imagination, fantasy, and, above all, by allowing them to change under your interested observation.

CHAPTER SIX

Hypnotic Work:
Attitude Control

Attitudes are mental positions regarding something
(person, place, idea, situation, or object). They are
powerful in their effects, and it is important to explore
them carefully and act on the insights you get. The
attitudes we will be concerned with are the ones that
bear on anything related to passing your exam or
meeting any other challenge.

Attitudes may be very firmly reality-based, entrenched
through interconnections with unconscious emotional
reactions and personal preferences, or instilled through
a lifetime of conditioning. On the other hand, they can
be tenuously based on minimal information or mis-
understandings.

In the process of exploring an attitude, whether it
is strong or weak, alternative ways of viewing the situation usually emerge. Very minor changes in the attitude

may obliterate its destructive effects. Constructive ways of dealing with the situation then easily come to mind.

Examples of Attitude Problems

Your attitude toward your exam might be: "I think the people who made up the state licensing exam for————must be sadists. It is miserable! I have failed it twice already and this is the last time I'm going to take it. I hate the bastards! The smart-ass monitors creeping around trying to catch people cheating don't help either."

This is a very strong hostile attitude toward the exam and the exam situation. However, you could still have a good attitude toward the *material* you have to learn. In that case, studying would be no problem. But with the attitude toward the examiners expressed in this example you would certainly have emotions that would get in the way of your exam performance. To handle them you should use techniques learned in the previous chapter.

An entirely different approach is needed with this attitude: "I just love art history. I study it all the time. I get carried away following up some obscure artifact that no one ever heard of. I know I shouldn't do that now. I have to memorize these tons of dates and junk for the exam or I'll *never* get to be an art historian. But I can't keep my mind on the things I know the test will cover because I keep getting enmeshed in some fascinating detail."

This is a much more positive attitude but no less destructive of good exam-passing behavior. However, the trouble during the exam is not emotional. It is mental. You simply would not have the information you need to pass the exam because you hadn't studied properly. The solution would be to develop mental control during your study period. You will learn the techniques for this in the next chapter.

In both these examples very little exploration and analysis was needed to decide what action to take for reducing the destructiveness of these attitudes. In these cases, the major effort must be put into applying the solutions. The next couple of vignettes show the importance of careful exploration of the attitude in order to bring unconscious aspects into awareness.

A married woman was trying to get a job so her husband could go back to school, but she was unable to meet the challenge. She continually failed job interviews, aptitude tests, and so on. While exploring her attitudes hypnotically she discovered an unconscious aspect of her attitude that had motivated her failure.

Unconsciously she had thought, "If my husband gets a Ph.D. he will be too educated for me and will get bored with me. As a professor he will meet charming, sophisticated women and will leave me for one of them."

Consciously she really wanted her husband to become a professor. The life of academia appealed to her but she realized that she needed preparation for becoming a professor's wife. Their solution was for both of them to work part time and both go back to school. He became a professor, and she became a charming, sophisticated woman, confident in her ability to hold a good job and her husband.

A young woman who was majoring in languages demonstrates further complexities. In her second semester of French she became unable to learn the language and was flunking her tests regularly. Her attitude was: "I love languages, and especially the Romance languages. I can't imagine why I have suddenly started blocking on French. It just doesn't make sense."

In deep hypnosis something entirely different emerged. She had a sudden recall of a scene in which her instructor made a sexual overture to her at the end of the first semester. She was very upset and completely repressed the event. The reasons for her repression were complex and had to do with her recent marriage failure and her sexual conditioning in an emotionally tumultuous childhood.

But it was not necessary to pursue the reasons. As soon as she remembered the instructor's seductive behavior she could state an unconscious aspect of her attitude.

"I cannot handle an affair with a married man. I am attracted to him, however, and I might not be able to resist if he approaches me again. I must not attract him. I will be an unattractive dummy. I will not be able to learn French. I have no right to the pleasure of Romance languages anyway. I am a failure in romance."

This kind of reasoning was silly to her rational, conscious mind. "Failing the course is no way to avoid attracting attention to myself. My instructor could even use this opportunity to insist on giving me individual tutoring and make a new approach then. Whether I learn French and pass the course or not bears little on my having a confrontation with him again. I must handle that in some more adaptive way. And certainly learning French or any other Romance language need have nothing to do with my success in personal romance."

Becoming aware of all this was sufficient to change completely her study and test performance. She began to make excellent grades. The confidence she gained from her improvement carried over, and she felt she could handle any approach her instructor made. She was able to simplify the matter further by giving him subtle cues of her unavailability and had no more trouble with him or with her grades.

Exploring Your Attitudes

The foregoing examples should make clear the advantages of getting acquainted with your attitudes. Nevertheless, it takes courage to face them sometimes. Don't worry that they are "bad." The important thing is that you make them explicit, become aware of their unconscious aspects, and keep them from interfering with your work.

In the process of stating and exploring them you will discover many new aspects of your attitudes of which you were unaware. For example, you may find that your instructor reminds you of your ex-husband. Don't be concerned about how muddled, fragmented, or apparently irrelevant these unconscious aspects seem to be or embarrassed about how foolish, mean, sexual, or stupid they appear. You don't have to tell them to anybody else but *you* need to know them so you can do something about them. The more you know about yourself the better off you are.

Now turn on your recorder and ask yourself these questions aloud. Answer yourself as completely as you can. Respond to yourself just as if you were a friendly, nonjudgmental person interested in drawing someone out.

"What will be the advantages if you pass this exam? What will be the disadvantages if you pass? How will your life change? Who will benefit and in what ways? How will you feel about yourself if you pass?

"What will be the consequences if you don't pass? Who will speak to you about it? What will they say to you? What will you have to do as a result of failing? What excuses do you have for failing? How will you feel about yourself if you fail?

"How do you feel about the content of the course of study necessary to pass this exam? Is it important to you to know this material or to develop these skills other than to pass the exam? How do you feel about the instructor? How do you feel about the authors of the books you are studying? About the institution associated with the test?

"Is there more involved than meets the eye? Are you trying to prove something to yourself or someone else?

What? Who led you into taking this exam or into this field of interest? How?"

Listen to the recording you have just made. Make notes of the findings. Pick one of the attitudes and explore it hypnotically. For example: "I plan to explore my attitude toward the group I'm in that meets once a week to study for the state medical technology exam. I really like going to the group but I'm not learning much."

After you have picked the attitude you wish to explore and have written it out in detail, hypnotize yourself. Turn your recorder on, and after you are deep enough to focus well, go over all the ramifications of the attitude that will come to you. Record your thoughts, feelings, and memories. Follow them wherever they lead. Speak clearly, describing in detail what you are experiencing.

The outcome of the above plan might be: In a hypnotic state the man vividly recalled the meetings and found that he really wanted deeper friendships with the men in the group. But having no other contact with them he was using the meetings as a social occasion. He realized that he was annoying and alienating them with his lack of seriousness about studying. When he saw what he was doing he decided to set up get-togethers with them outside the meetings and to devote himself intensively to study during the meetings.

While still hypnotized he developed some ideas for effective learning and planned in detail what he would bring to the group the next week. He came out of the hypnotic state feeling very encouraged about learning what he needed to know and about making friends.

It is impossible to give examples that will be pertinent to everyone. Stretch your imagination to fill in for your particular situation and attitudes.

Explore your attitudes toward every aspect of the exam: the different topics (perhaps you love inorganic but hate organic chemistry and the exam will cover both), the exam taking itself, the different kinds of questions (multiple choice and essay), the instructor, the books, and so on.

There are three likely outcomes to your explorations:

1. Finding no problems
2. Finding problems and their solutions
3. Finding problems but no solutions

Sometimes, even after you have explored an attitude thoroughly, you won't be able to come up with new material (problems, solutions, or unconscious aspects) because the attitude is not important to the particular challenge you are concerned with. Good. You no longer need deal with that attitude.

In the process of exploring, you will naturally solve many problems, as the people in the above examples did. The solutions will mostly be in the form of decisions to improve the way you have been doing something or to change the way you've been thinking about something. Write them out in detail and plan to review them daily as long as they are pertinent. Give yourself hypnotic suggestions that you will use these solutions

in the best possible way. Reinforce the hypnotic suggestions every day.

At other times you will not be able to think of
how to solve a problem even after you clearly define it.
In this case, write the problem out as fully as you can.
Hypnotize yourself and get the following ideas across
in your best hypnotic patter:

"You are very open and receptive. Within you lies
the best possible answer to any problem that confronts
you. Here is a problem which you will take deep inside
yourself and solve without conscious interference. You
will bring the solution into consciousness in a workable
form whenever you need it."

State the problem clearly to yourself three times,
then go to sleep or rest deeply for a few minutes. Bring
yourself out and go on to the next task.

You have given the problem to your unconscious to
solve. It is an extreme delight to deliberately relinquish
it and then have an extraordinarily creative solution pop
into your head the next day. Your only obligation is to
act on the solution in a responsible and dependable
manner once it comes.

An example:

The problem: "On beautiful sunny days I can get
very little work done because my mind keeps running
outdoors."

The solution which pops up early in the morning
of the next beautiful day he planned to study: "Type
out on cards a list of material you must memorize. Take
the kids on a picnic, play volleyball, get some sun, have
a good time. Pull out a card occasionally and run the

material through your head. Check yourself to see when you have it memorized and then start on the next card."

This solution not only permitted him to get out on pretty days but solved the problem of committing a long list to memory, a task he had been avoiding.

Before beginning the next chapter take a few minutes to review how you did with this one. What was your attitude toward working on your attitudes? Were you thorough? Did you get bored? Did you get carried away with some detail and spend an inordinate amount of time on it? Make notes of this appraisal and use your observations to perpetuate the successes and avoid the mistakes in the future.

CHAPTER SEVEN

Hypnotic Work:
Control of Mental Activity

Mental activity is the immediate experience you are aware of, including the intensity of each aspect and its flow or movement through your mind. For example, right now you are most aware of the concept of mental activity. You are drawing ideas and experiences from your past in an attempt to make it a clear and usable concept. You are remembering what you have read and heard about it before, what you think it means, how thoughts go through your mind and so on.

You are also aware, but to a lesser degree, that you are sitting in your chair, that your eyes are seeing black and white pages, that it is Sunday afternoon, that you are getting hungry perhaps. Good mental control requires that the awarenesses irrelevant to your immediate task consume a minimum of your attention.

Control of mental activity cannot be achieved by

fighting with yourself. Just as you can't force your hand to float, neither can you force your mind to perform the way you want it to. You can, however, *allow* it to perform in a most magnificent way.

Imagine your mind totally focused on whatever task you are carrying out, effectively learning in a flash, producing brilliant ideas, developing complete plans for carrying them out, able to recall so clearly that you feel you are living a remembered experience, able to fantasize so vividly that you can experience virtually anything in your imagination, able to lay thoughts aside so that you are never bothered by those not pertinent to what you are doing.

How to Respect Your Mind

The first thing that becomes clear when you reflect a moment on mental activity is that the mind is a busy, noisy beehive. When you try to concentrate you are usually annoyed with any thoughts that intrude and try to drive them away forcefully. This results in their rapid return and the battle is on. Or, just as troublesome to good concentration, you may fail to notice that an irrelevant thought has seduced you and you "come to" at the end of a page not knowing what you've read.

Rather than scolding yourself every time your mind wanders from the task at hand, note the wanderings. When you are studying have a pad beside you and make note of every distracting thought. Start now as you are reading this. These things we disparagingly call distractions are actually important and deserve your undivided attention later. By writing them down you postpone their return, and you are alerted to them so they can't captivate your attention unknowingly.

There are four types of thoughts you will find on your list:

1. Things you can take care of at the next break
2. Things you can take care of later
3. Things that need more thought but no action
4. Things that need no further concern

Your purpose is to keep your study period devoted as much as possible to study. You will certainly save yourself a lot of trouble and find some good ideas by noting the formerly annoying thoughts. But the main reason is that noting them during study periods keeps them from coming back to disturb your concentration or from sneakily stealing your mind away.

Go over the list every hour or so. Pick out the things you can immediately take care of and do so. Examples of these are: "thirsty, full bladder, picture hanging crooked."

Decide what action is necessary for each of the things you can take care of later and set the best time to carry it out. Examples of these are: "send thank-you note, return library books, call Mary, build gate for back-yard." Be realistic in planning to do these things. Check yourself over a period of time to see how accurate you were in your expectations of yourself. Improve your judgment with experience. The more dependable you are, the more apt your mind is to remain clear. Just as a wife will nag a husband who says, "I'll do it in a minute," but doesn't, so your mind will nag you if you put it off.

If a particular thought continues to recur but is the kind of thing you can take no action on, spend some time at your break dealing with it internally. If emotions are motivating the persistent thoughts, the techniques for handling emotions are applicable. Usually a vividly experienced hypnotic fantasy alone is sufficient to prevent the thought from recurring. If not, the hypnotic fantasy will usually lead to creative ideas on handling the problem. This may involve creative altruism.

Creative altruism is thinking up and doing something helpful which is related to the bothersome thought. For example, suppose you honked at a blind man before you realized he was blind and can't stop thinking about the hurt expression on his face. Reading to a blind person for an hour is a sure way to clear your mind.

If a popular song or ditty keeps running through your head, you can get rid of it by replacing it for awhile with a more complex piece of music. Since the complex piece requires more effort to maintain, it disappears shortly and the other doesn't usually return.

Many things on the list will not need action. They will be observations, worries, regrets, expectations: "My, that flower is pretty! I sure am proud of my baby! I hope it doesn't rain the day of the ball game. I'm sorry I threw those notes away. I bet the ice skating exhibition is really going to be good." Of course, you shouldn't take time to write them out in such detail. Just jot a word in each case to remind you.

As you develop this receptive attitude toward distracting thoughts, you will find that some thoughts trip so lightly through your mind that they don't really distract you. Leave them unrecorded. Since they aren't interfering they needn't concern you.

If you take these steps, you will find that not only the specific things you've taken care of, but distracting thoughts in general will stop nagging for your attention. It seems that your respectful attitude quiets your mind. It shows that you don't consider yourself a scatterbrain who is harassed by ridiculous thoughts but a person with many clear ideas that deserve to be put into action.

Naturally with this attitude you will attend to your ideas intelligently and dependably and act on them with confidence. When you have built up trust in yourself, the ideas will not need to clamor for attention. You will find that when you address yourself to one task the other tasks will wait their turn because, to speak metaphorically, they know their turn will come and they will get your full attention. Your mind will be clear and concentrated and able to learn quickly whatever you devote it to.

Hypnotic Helps with Mental Control

There are two principle ways to use the hypnotic state for getting things done:

1. Perform the required task while in the hypnotic state
2. Use the hypnotic state to give suggestions about your performance later

The tasks that can usefully be done in the hypnotic state are limited by two conditions:

1. How much sensory input is necessary
2. How important a critical attitude is

If the task requires too much sensory input it is difficult to stay in the hypnotic state. Many people can't stay in self-hypnosis with their eyes open.

When you are hypnotized you do not have your usual degree of critical faculties about you. If the task involves new material it is desirable to appraise it critically first. For example, you have to decide what is important enough to learn, or you might need to learn something by rote but want to make a point of not believing it. These decisions should be made in ordinary consciousness. Also, you usually need to consider new material in light of other things you know, to compare and contrast, and so on. This is also better done for the first time in the waking state. Hypnosis is not useful in studying most material at the initial reading.

You have already found how very useful it is to be in a hypnotic state when reviewing your past, seeking creative ideas, searching for the nuances of feelings, reviewing unconscious aspects of attitudes, and such things. You will find it equally valuable for the intellectual task of reviewing familiar material inside your head. It is ideal for this purpose because you can do the reviewing with your eyes closed and lying perfectly still. It calls for an active process of bringing the information into consciousness, which is very valuable for thorough learning. Besides, for the sake of your self-confidence, you need to know that the material is actually inside your mind. People often review by going over and over notes. This only increases anxiety.

You readily see the growth of your hypnotic skill over time when you use hypnosis for review. You will also experience differences in your effectiveness at different depths of hypnosis. In a very light hypnotic state you will find your review of material somewhat superior to merely thinking about it in ordinary consciousness. At very deep levels you will eventually be able to visualize your notes and review the material just as if you were looking at it. However, even after you master visualizing your notes in deep hypnosis you should occasionally review at light levels of hypnosis and in the waking state also. This is to assure that you will not have to hypnotize yourself deeply during the exam in order to get access to the material.

But do not dismiss the possible use of deep hypnosis in an emergency. Once during an essay exam I drew a complete blank on one of the questions. There was a good emotional reason for this, but I didn't have time to be concerned with that. I only wanted to get the information and write a satisfactory answer. I was very highly motivated because a proudly maintained straight A average hinged on this question. I hypnotized myself deeply, visualized the book, flipped through and found the information, read it, came out of hypnosis, and wrote the answer.

This was most difficult under the pressure and a little embarrassing since my instructor and classmates knew of my interest in hypnosis and it was obvious what I was doing. I highly recommend that you solve your emotional problems before the exam and have all the information more easily accessible.

In using the hypnotic state for giving yourself suggestions about later performance, you already know to use compelling instructions, repetition, and imaginative imagery. All these are especially important in suggesting mental control. Since the mind itself is so tricky, it is important to use every device you know in dealing with it. The more vigorously you give instructions, the more you repeat them; the more imaginative your imagery, the greater will be the response of your mind. In addition, the use of symbols and implied and indirect suggestions will reach different levels of your mind and increase the effectiveness of your suggestions.

In order to clear your mind you might use the image of ocean waves washing away footprints, sand writing, and half-destroyed sand castles, leaving behind smooth, white, sparkling sand. Imagine the smoothness of the sand reflecting the clarity of your mind.

Decide what you want to accomplish and have a list of suggestions in mind at all times. To get creative ideas for imaginative suggestions use direct suggestions that you will get such ideas.

Hypnotize yourself now and review this chapter in your mind. Relate what has been said here to your own experience. See how vividly you can recall the actual words that were used. Try it at different depths of hypnosis. Explore your attitudes toward the chapter. Then hypnotically review the material again. See if you can recall it any better. Before you come out of hypnosis give suggestions that you will do even better on the next task.

Record on tape what you are reviewing in your mind. When you come out of the hypnotic state compare your memory as revealed on the tape with the actual material in the book. Don't become discouraged because you don't do well enough to suit yourself, but don't settle for too little. You will continue to learn this particular skill every day and you will see your skill develop daily.

Now repeat what you just did with this chapter using an earlier chapter that you haven't read for several hours. The purpose of this review is to study the process and to practice it. Use everything you have learned so far this weekend to help you in meeting the challenge of learning to use hypnosis for intellectual review. The next section offers a further technique which will prove invaluable for reviewing material.

Time Distortion

Your experience of the movement of time is usually pretty closely related to the movements of the hands of the clock. However, the accuracy with which you judge the passage of time depends on conditioning, effort, and changes in your state of consciousness.

You have had dreams in which things happen that would take a long time when in actuality only a few seconds have passed. This proves that the mind is capable of tremendous "speed," and, in the dream state at least, of tremendous time distortion. Our waking expectations hold us fairly rigidly to a standard pace of time.

In very deep hypnosis a thoroughly trained and experienced person can have the imagined experience of playing a thirty-minute piano piece in only a few seconds of clock time. This can be just as beneficial as a half-hour of practice.

You must, however, be more modest in your goals at this point. If you can make your study time subjectively longer, even to a small degree, you will get correspondingly more benefit from it.

Time is a very confusing thing and confusion leads to time distortion, so most anything you can say to yourself about time may serve your purpose. Don't even try to understand the process of distorting time. A method that seems logical at the moment may make more sense when completely reversed the next time you think about it. Simply keep records of the results of different approaches to see which works best for you.

Don't be discouraged if you aren't able to make much headway in slowing your experience of time in the few hours that remain this weekend. Your ability will increase with practice just as will all your other hypnotic skills.

There are two basic approaches to distorting time in the direction useful for study and exam taking. You can give suggestions that time is slowing down or that you are speeding up. Of course, the only time you can influence is subjective time so if you can get control over your time perceiving mechanism you can lengthen time that way. Or, if you can pack more living into each moment by getting more done, thinking faster, living more fully, time will seem to have slowed as a result.

The success with which you can make these ideas really affect your mind is dependent on your ingenuity. Study yourself in relation to time. Change your maladaptive attitudes toward it such as: "I'm always late. I never have time for anything. I don't know where the time goes."

If necessary ferret out the roots of the emotional problems underlying the attitudes. For example, you may have identified with a parent who had similar attitudes. Or, if you have a spouse who is always early, rigidly scheduled, and so forth, this could provoke you to provide balance in the relationship by going too far the other way.

After a hypnotic session in which you thoroughly explore your attitudes and deal with them in whatever way seems useful, give yourself time distorting suggestions in a deep hypnotic state. The following model, together with the discoveries you make in your attitude work, can serve to help you develop your patter.

"As you go deeper and deeper and deeper feel yourself becoming more and more disoriented in time, forgetting what day it is, what month it is, what year it is, forgetting what time it is, whether it is daylight or dark. Let go of your time sense, just as you have let go of your sense of sight by letting your eyes lock shut. Let go of 'the eyes of time.'

"Go deeper and deeper into a hypnotic state, way, way down. It is not hard to let go of your awareness of time. In fact, it's hard to hold on because time is such a bewildering, confusing, incomprehensible thing—very, very strange. It seems to move, or do we move through it? Does it flow by like a river passing by us, or do we move through it like walking through molasses or running through still air? Yes, sometimes we walk through time as if it were cold molasses—hardly able to move, to get anywhere, to get anything done.

"At other times (voice speeding up) we whiz through time as if it were light, buoyant, falling, falling through time, faster and faster and faster. It is a vacuum and you are plummeting through it; drawn by the force of gravity, falling through time, drawn more and more quickly, so very fast.

(Voice abruptly assuming normal speed) "Then again we can forget about time. It passes. We don't care how fast or how slowly; we just let it go. But now, right now, you are going to capture time, this most precious time.

"You will do this simply by letting your mind function efficiently, effectively, and rapidly. You will experience time in a new way so that when you look at the clock you will be startled to see that so little time has passed. Back to work after having glanced at the clock, you will be confident that you will finish what you have to do because you have sooo much time. All those precious moments to use, to use, to use—those precious moments—strings of precious moments extending forever."

And so forth. You can go on and on suggesting to yourself in an infinity of ways. Experiment, experiment, and experiment again. It is not easy to get extreme time distortion through self-hypnosis, but any amount is worth the effort.

CHAPTER EIGHT

Application of Hypnotic Skills

There are two major focuses involved in applying your hypnotic skills to meeting your challenge: first is learning what you need to know, and second is applying your knowledge. This last evening of the weekend you will use your hypnotic skills to develop an ongoing program that takes into consideration the specifics you must learn, your personality type, and the particular life circumstances under which you must work.

You have learned to use hypnosis to: get in touch with and change emotions, discover and change conscious and unconscious attitudes, respect your mind, focus your attention, distort time, and allow creative emergence of ideas. No matter how capable you are with self-hypnosis or how enthusiastic you presently are, your ultimate success hinges specifically on whether you continue to use it to deal with the problems facing

you. To insure future persistence you will hypnotize
yourself four times this evening to work out the ideal
program for *you*.

To simplify the presentation in this chapter I will
assume as an example that you are a student who has
a formal exam to pass. First, begin by considering the
exam itself. Second, take a thorough look at the human
factors, *you*. Third, review your life circumstances.
Finally, create the best program you can design with
enough room for flexibility so that it adjusts itself
to fit your changing needs.

What will the exam or challenge actually call on
you to do? Don't focus on the volumes to be covered
or the hours you must practice. It will do you no good
to read libraries if the reading doesn't increase your
exam-passing ability. Read to learn, not to cover
material.

Do you have to be able to answer true-false questions
on material taken from a number of books? Must you
take an engine apart and put it back together, program
a computer, work algebra problems from a certain
book, type sixty words a minute with no more than
three errors per page, discuss legal cases in writing,
make an oral presentation, recognize paintings of
various artists, have general knowledge of some field?
Find out all you can about the exam from inside your
head now and from other sources later.

In order to learn specifics it is important to construct
the list of skills you need to develop for passing the
exam. The ability to write the correct answers to certain
questions can be considered a skill and *that* is the skill

you need now. When you hypnotize yourself in a few minutes record everything that comes to mind concerning the skills you need. Focus your attention entirely on the exam. Imagine you are the exam maker and see what kind of questions you construct. Visualize the exam and see what the questions are.

Use every device you can think of to get the most possible information about it. When you have concluded to your satisfaction, bring yourself out. Then listen to the tape and write a list of the skills you will develop. After the weekend you can amplify the list by referring to your books and other material. This list is the key to your quick, thorough learning.

Now you are ready to hypnotize yourself. As soon as you are in a hypnotic state and receptive to suggestions, emphasize to yourself that you will never again force yourself to study a certain amount of time. Instead you will willingly, if not eagerly, study to learn specifics you want to know.

Use a composite of your hypnotic skills and thoroughly deal with the questions raised in this section. You will end up with a good basic understanding of your feelings and attitudes toward the learning of the specifics and a list of skills to develop.

Human Factors—You

In the next hypnotic session you will focus on yourself. The desired outcome is that you emerge with as much self-acceptance as possible. Acceptance comes from understanding, so open yourself to seeing your obviously positive qualities fully and search for value in the qualities you usually consider negative.

The use of the personality types can serve as a guide though you are much more complex than any analysis can ever show. Begin by reviewing the qualities of your type.

If you are *Type I,* you tend to skip merrily through the basic stages of skill development and get in trouble later because you haven't built a firm foundation. Forewarned, you avoided allowing this to interfere with your hypnotic development so far. Since you are a fast learner you may be able to browse lightly over certain information and yet retain it. To avoid trouble later simply test yourself before proceeding further. In this way you will guarantee a firm foundation while respecting your intuitive grasp of the basics.

One of your greatest advantages is your receptivity to hypnotic suggestion. Be sure to make full use of this.

Consider ways to make use of your spontaneity. Perhaps you can make it the basis of most of your learning. In the next section you will hear about how to steal moments that would otherwise be wasted. With your particular personality and hypnotic ability you may be able to learn much by grabbing brief periods that unexpectedly occur and using them well.

If you are *Type II,* learning hypnosis has probably been a slower process. In this chapter you come to an area where you have a special competence. You know how to plan a program and how to stick with it. Your tendency is to make it so rigorous that your human limitations of time and energy catch up with you. Be kind and generous with yourself. Don't forget to allow for all the other needs you have. Don't forget fun and relaxation too. "All work and no play . . ."

If you are *Type III,* you should be specially conscientious in the next hypnotic session. You are available for rapid changes within yourself and are therefore not easy to predict. You may want to study especially hard at certain times and review only briefly when your interest temporarily turns to something else. If you continue to use hypnosis daily you can succeed because of this very quality. You can take advantage of your remarkable energy when it becomes available to you and not begrudge your energy lag. Remember to allow. Don't try to force.

Now, whatever your type, hypnotize yourself and spend the session reviewing your personal qualities. Focus on your strengths and how you can design your study program to take full advantage of them. See if you can become creative enough to find ways that your so-called weaknesses can add to your success. Record your findings as you go along and when you come out make careful notes.

Life Circumstance

The purpose of the next hypnotic session is to review your life circumstance and discover what you can change in order to make more time and energy available for self-hypnosis and study. Most people overcommit themselves. A chronic cry is, "I don't have time!"

Many of the commitments are habitual and unnecessary. For instance, some people spend many hours buying, preparing, and eating food. A woman commented to me that the most outstanding thing she noticed when she fasted for a few days was the inordinate amount of time she had on her hands.

Find things you are willing to lay aside temporarily until you pass your exam. Would you be willing to forgo your predinner cocktail and substitute relaxing with self-hypnosis? Stop watching TV? Stop reading the paper? Reduce the standards of cleanliness for your house?

You will detect all manner of ways to save time and energy. During the hypnosis session record ways to change. Perhaps you can get the kids off to school without the emotional drain that yelling and screaming entails, clean the breakfast dishes more quickly, use hypnosis to relax instead of lingering over cigarettes and coffee. Or, at the office you might bring a glass of water to your desk and avoid the chitchat at the cooler.

Routine work that doesn't demand mental effort offers opportunity for study. Forget such proclamations as, "I will study all weekend" or "I will stay up all night for three nights before the exam." These are unrealistic and inefficient ways of dealing with time for study. A much better way is to have a clear-cut goal of developing a skill or acquiring a set of facts and to grab time the moment you are ready to work. Keep in mind the maxim, "Be in the Now," and studying will become an exciting, rewarding experience.

Let's concretize. You have ten minutes to wait for your bus and a twenty-minute ride—a wonderful opportunity. Suppose you know that to pass your exam you must be able to list all the essential amino acids and their importance in the body. Don't be disturbed that you don't have your book or notes with you. The skill for passing the exam isn't the ability to read a book but the ability to bring the material from inside your head.

Self-consciousness may pose a problem here, but you have hypnosis to deal with the self-consciousness. Tell yourself you couldn't care less what people think. Closed eyes and relaxed muscles are common enough on public transportation. But, even though there is no law against it, letting your hand float might draw a crowd. If this presents a problem just imagine that your hand is floating but hold it down. You will go into a hypnotic state anyway. Recall a time when you were studying the amino acids. Bring them to mind one by one and fill in as much information as possible.

Let your eyes open occasionally so that you can catch the right bus and get off at your stop. After thirty minutes of such intense review you will unquestionably know the amino acids you were able to recall and will be eager to learn those you missed.

One of the major values in this kind of study is that it creates an intense desire to fill in the blank spaces in your mind. There will not be the slightest problem in finding time for this. It is even likely that you will skip lunch and go to the library at noon to look up the information.

Focus your attention on learning rather than just on *spending time* studying and the problem of procrastination ceases to exist. You want to study because you can see the immediate change in your knowledge which results.

Now use the above ideas as the stimulus for a deep hypnotic session in which you determine the aspects of your life that need to be considered and/or revised in designing your hypnotic program of study. Begin with a typical day. How much of it do you really enjoy? How much of what you do is useful and necessary? Review your life in minute detail. Record every idea that might lead to finding more time or more energy. When you come out make careful notes.

The Exam Situation

Before you make your final plan you should have in mind the most effective method for dealing with examination anxiety. The use of this method should be included in your program.

When you actually go to the exam you want it to seem so familiar that you will feel as if it has already been successfully completed. Here is how to prepare yourself: Every day hypnotize yourself and experience the exam situation as clearly and vividly as possible in your imagination. The moment you feel any anxiety go back to hand levitation and relaxation suggestions to get yourself calm and relaxed again. After that return to the exam. You may go back and forth many times each session.

Imagine every detail. If you know the room, conjure it up. Imagine the desk, your pencil and paper, your clothing, and the feeling of calmness and confidence you have. This is also a perfect opportunity to review in the best possible way. Read the exam through in your imagination. Study it and the answers you give.

The night before the exam go to bed early, hypnotize yourself, and suggest good, restful sleep. Avoid cramming. This just increases anxiety and wastes energy. Reassure yourself by bringing material into consciousness; that is, review in your head and practice recall.

The day of the exam you should arrive a few minutes early, hypnotize yourself, and vividly imagine that you are calmly taking the exam. Tell yourself that you will be totally focused on the exam, and that nothing will distract you. When you get the exam, read through it if possible. Earlier answers are often hidden in the phrasing of later questions. Do not be concerned about answering the questions until you have read all the way through. Just read for information. Now go back to the beginning and work your way through again, answering the easy ones first and the more difficult ones later.

If you have a propensity toward stubbornness beware of spending too much time on any particular question at the expense of others. In your daily hypnotic work with the exam situation, imagine yourself avoiding this pitfall, finding hidden answers, and generally having a good time.

Designing Your Program

Get your notes together from the last three hypnotic sessions and read them over. The program you design will have to be a very individual one, but the following check points may be helpful.

Does it include:

Sufficient use of motivating suggestions
Use of time that would otherwise be wasted
Allowance for time with family and friends
Focus on specifics
Both brief, light hypnosis and long, deep sessions
Taking advantage of your altered state on awakening
Use of the private time just before sleeping
Flexibility?

Hypnotize yourself and visualize the design of your program. Record your ideas and after coming out of hypnosis write them out. Use your notes. When you are satisfied wtih your program get a good night's sleep. When you awaken start your daily routine with an attitude of experimentation.

If you successfully include flexibility in your program, you can always modify it to fit your needs. If the program becomes unpleasant in any way, change it. You guarantee success when you use hypnosis to facilitate what works for you.

CHAPTER NINE

Other Challenges

After you have successfully used this book to pass exams you will certainly want to continue to use it to meet other challenges. If you have no exams to pass you will want to apply self-hypnosis to the challenges you do have. In this chapter I will assume that you have already used the book to pass exams and are now available for ideas about approaching such challenges as:

Developing and breaking habits
Getting rid of maladies
Controlling pain
Learning skills for pleasure

To meet any and all challenges that can be included under these groups, you need the skills you learned in using the pendulum, discovering your type, inducing hypnosis, deepening the state, controlling emotions and attitudes, and developing mental control. The experience you gained in working out your study program will also be useful.

In addition, in order to meet most other challenges, you need to become adept in inducing and removing sensations, controlling autonomic functions, and manipulating your beliefs.

In dealing with emotions in Chapter Five, you developed the ability to control nervousness, butterflies, tightness, and other sensations that make up the emotions with which you worked. From this experience you have a notion of how to develop control of sensations.

You need to control sensations very precisely to meet some challenges. For example, if you want to stop overeating it is helpful to be able to hallucinate specific tastes and to control hunger and the vague sensations associated with food cravings.

Pain is pure sensation but it varies in degree of specificity and quality. It may be sharp or dull, precisely located or generalized. Learning to control pain is helpful in dealing with some maladies and all injuries. It is also helpful in the development of skills in which pain is an impediment. Pain control is useful for dancers during stretching exercises, for athletes during rough contact sports, for beginning musicians before the right callouses and muscular strength is developed, and so forth.

If the challenge you face is to get rid of certain maladies, control of autonomic functions is essential. You have already learned some autonomic control. You learned to flush and blanch in hypnotically induced anger and fear. This is beginning control of circulation. With this ability you can facilitate healing by directing blood flow to the body parts involved.

To deal with some maladies you may need to develop control of heart rate, secretion of gastric juice, mobility of the intestinal tract, and so on. Do not be concerned that you will cause trouble due to your ignorance of body processes. You are not developing conscious control at the cost of unconscious control. What you are actually doing is removing impediments to ideal functioning so that the wisdom of the body can take over fully.

You manipulated your beliefs when you convinced yourself that your eyelids were heavy, would close automatically, and would lock shut. Likewise, with getting your hand to float. These experiences aided you in convincing yourself that you would be calm and focused during your exams and at study time.

Another belief that is of great value is that you have hidden talents which are emerging. The belief may be very tenuous at first but as it brings about improvements it is reinforced. In this way your step-by-step accomplishments lend support to your belief. Strong belief assists the emergence of your talents.

Habits

There are innumerable ways you may want to change. You may want to become a nonsmoker, stop overeating, be even-tempered, have a positive outlook, be prompt, be well organized, remember people's names. Or you may not really want to change but really *wish* you wanted to change.

In this latter case the first thing to do is to use hypnotic suggestions to bring about a desire to improve in some particular way. Even if you already have a desire to break or develop a habit, it is a good idea to enhance that desire continually. Besides giving direct suggestions of increased desire, go over all the reasons for change in vivid detail.

In a deep hypnotic state let the increased freedom of contact with your memory banks and creativity lead you to find reasons that wouldn't normally have occurred to you.

In the process of doing this your belief in yourself will naturally grow. Facilitate this growth with direct suggestions. "You are as certain to stop smoking as the sun is to rise. There is no way you will continue to smoke. Just as you can't possibly get your eyes open now you can't possibly resist becoming a nonsmoker."

In addition to giving direct suggestions use visualization of yourself being the way you want to be and reaping the benefits of your new state.

When you have decided to take a definite step toward bringing about the change, take yourself into a deep hypnotic state and review the origin of the habit in question. If you aren't able to remember the beginning, just go back as far as you can with clear memories and then go back to the beginning and make up scenes that could reasonably have occurred. In the process of doing this the main thing to look for are needs that motivated you.

For example, in reviewing your early cigarette smoking you may find that three things motivated you: to be one of the crowd, to feel grown-up, and to appear sophisticated.

Now check out whether any of these needs are still current. It will simplify matters if the crowd has changed and most of the members don't smoke, if you *are* grown up now, and if appearing sophisticated no longer appeals to you. In that case, you need give the original motives no further concern.

On the other hand, suppose that as a result of current pressures you find yourself in the process of developing habits you really don't want to have. Do you find yourself taking tokes on joints just because they are being passed around when you don't really want to get stoned? Are you drinking a little more booze or beer each week because of social situations? Or because of pressure at work are you taking a little longer to unwind over predinner cocktails? Are you developing the habit of nagging your children as they get to the age in which they leave their things lying around?

Or are you losing some good habit you wanted to maintain? Had you walked to work for years and really benefited from it but now find yourself inclined to take a free ride since your new neighbor offers it?

In a hypnotic state review all the possibilities that come to you. Use your creativity to come up with answers that fill the bill. Find more adaptive ways to satisfy these original motives and put them into practice.

Next, find out what additional motives have arisen in the time you have been engaging in the habit. Because of the pressure of the moment it is difficult to introspect as an habitual act is about to occur. I have found that cigarette smokers who may otherwise be very articulate and in tune with their feelings are unable to elucidate what makes them want a cigarette. Habitual naggers, criticizers, and put-down artists constantly lament, "I don't know why I said that. It's just second nature."

By using hypnosis to gain distance and perspective you will be able to develop understanding. Recall a time when you let the pressure build before giving in to your habit. Find out in detail exactly what sensations, thoughts, irritations, pleasures, emotions, and attitudes motivated you to engage in the habit.

Once you have determined what they are, develop ways to bring them on and take them away. Use what you have already learned about hypnotic control in creative ways.

You may want to use hypnotic imagery of yourself engaging in the habit and fulfill your desire in this way while you are getting used to your new self *sans* habit. In the process you will be learning how to evoke the sensations and take them away. For instance, with smoking you should be able to bring on the dry throat, tight chest, incipient tremulousness, and take them away by imaging a cigarette in your mouth. Focus on the feeling of the touch between your lips, the taste, the sound of the match or lighter, and so forth.

In a hypnotic state go over in your mind what environmental changes will facilitate your breaking the habit. You might consider more sleep and exercise, better diet, new friends, less TV. See what you come up with and arrange your life accordingly. Throughout your program, and even after you have given up the habit completely, continue to instill confidence that you will maintain your new state.

Maladies

The first thing to consider in dealing with a malady is whether you have a predisposition to get the disease because of your attitudes. Did your parents have this trouble? Did a doctor suggest you were likely to get it? Did you get the idea you were susceptible to it from something you read? Use hypnosis to discover and remove these attitudes just as you did your destructive attitudes toward exams and study.

Look for precipitating events that brought it on. Had you been overworking? Were you under a strain? Had some tragedy befallen you? Or, for that matter, had you had some great relief? Sudden positive changes also cause susceptibility. Find out about these and take care of them if possible. As a preventative measure, you should give your body extra care during times of stress. Take any actions that will relieve your mind of some nagging obligation. Get help when there is too much work. Do whatever you can to reduce the destructive effect of stress.

Next, note what benefits you get from having the problem. Do you get to take off from work? Do you enjoy your visits to the doctor because he is so nice to you? Do you get sympathy? Do you like feeling sorry for yourself? Are you getting financial compensation? Find out what the rewards are and give them to yourself without the necessity for illness if possible.

I have a friend who virtually eliminated childhood diseases, colds, and upset stomachs among her children by making a policy that they could stay home from school two days a month without being sick. Do the same for yourself. When you can't give yourself the benefits of the illness convince yourself that the benefits are less valuable than good health.

Even if you no longer benefit from having a malady, your body may have developed the habit of continuing it. One friend suffered severe menstrual cramps every month for which she took strong pain medication. When she was an adolescent she had a cold and demanding mother who, nevertheless, was kind and sympathetic with her during her cramps and let her stay home from school. As an adult she received no gains from the cramps but her body had gotten into the habit of cramping during menstruation. In a hypnotic state she recalled how important her mother's kindness was to her at those times and realized this had brought on the condition. During the hypnotic session she convinced her body to stop the cramping habit. The cramps never recurred except briefly one time when her mother visited during a menstrual period.

Extensive research has been done on the psychological aspects of diseases classified as psychosomatic. Some kinds of ulcers and some arthritic conditions are probably the best researched. The essence of the conclusions in these two syndromes is that the ulcer person is trying to be mature and independent, which involves making difficult decisions, while at a deeper level feeling insecure and dependent. The arthritic is supposed to have difficulty in expressing angry feelings satisfactorily. If you can maintain a good attitude toward the efforts of the researchers to understand the psychosomatic aspects of a disease, a thorough reading of the literature on your particular malady may be useful.

By reading up on asthma and discovering that most asthmatics had overprotected childhoods, a student of mine got ideas about how to treat his asthma. He cured it by taking hypnotic trips back into childhood and dealing with his overprotective mother in new ways. I didn't even know he had done this until he came back months later and asked if he could use hypnosis to get his asthma back because he was about to be drafted. He had braces put on his teeth instead.

By considering psychological aspects a friend cleared up a vaginal infection. In a hypnotic state she realized that it was serving to frustrate her husband who was in turn frustrating her by his unwillingness to engage in enough foreplay before intercourse. When she realized what was happening she decided to deal with the sexual problem directly without having to suffer the discomfort of the vaginal infection. She suggested that her body would do whatever was necessary to clear up the infection and she would do whatever was necessary to clear up the sexual difficulty. After a heart-to-heart talk with her husband and a willingness on her part to be a little more assertive during sex the infection cleared up. Prior to this discovery she had gone to her gynecologist and tried standard treatments.

Another woman cured herself of an ulcer without actually solving any psychological problem but by influencing herself through fantasy. She had thoroughly trained herself in hypnosis and knew the power of hypnotic fantasy. In a hypnotic state she came up with the idea that a skin graft over her ulcer would protect it while it healed. She had had successful skin surgery in actuality and was familiar with the process. In self-hypnosis she went through detailed two-hour surgery in her mind and imagined a skin graft over the ulcer. In reality this would not work because a skin graft wouldn't take in the stomach. Nevertheless, her positive feelings about it served to stimulate a healing process that led to immediate removal of ulcer symptoms and quick and complete recovery.

During her hypnotic work she also gave some thought to reducing stomach acidity and activity and to being calmer. Just the fact that she would go through such a detailed process suggests she was intently focused on healing. Her verbalized and/or visualized suggestions of healing got through to those aspects of her self which take care of such things.

This woman's work with her malady is a move in the

direction of focus on the physiological reactions which make up the disease. If your psychological approach doesn't solve your problem, turn your attention to the physical aspects.

Think of your malady as a habit you have of responding in a maladaptive way. One difference between maladies and ordinary habits is that you don't usually question yourself about it. It would seem strange to say, "I should quit this silly sneezing just because a cat comes into the room." Or, "I don't know why I had to secrete all that acid and get my ulcer bleeding again just because my boss bawled me out. That's a dumb thing to do."

One reason you wouldn't be apt to make such comments is that you feel so helpless in developing control over these kinds of functions. It is difficult to know what you are doing inside your stomach or nose or chest. It is difficult to change what is going on there at will. In order to do so you have to do what I call *expanding the volitional self.* You have to think, "*I* did it," instead of, "my body did it." If you know that taking responsibility just means you have the power to change what you yourself created it isn't at all odious. To get the feeling of response ability, the ability to respond the way you want to, you must first expand your awareness. Hypnotic focus, as you have already discovered, helps immensely. An additional, big help is the use of biofeedback equipment. In the last several years, electronic measuring instruments have been fitted for use in giving feedback to a person about his own physiological changes.

In learning to revivify emotions you inadvertantly

learned some control of circulation when you paled or reddened. This was helpful in showing you that you are capable of dilating and constricting your capillaries, but more precision is necessary to make this ability useful. You must become capable of directing blood flow to different areas of the body. Fortunately, there is a direct correlation between temperature of an area and the amount of blood flow in it so an electronic thermo-couple or thermometer can be used to give you informa-tion about blood flow change.

By imagining the body part being in warm water or under warm blankets you can bring about initial temperature changes. With the temperature feedback it is then usually sufficient merely to see the temperature change to learn to continue the change. In other words, you respond to the information without the necessity of using fantasy.

The development of this ability facilitates healing in all injuries and in many diseases. The ability to constrict blood vessels can be life saving in accidents where excess bleeding could occur. A less obvious application is in the control of headaches. Many headaches are the result of too much or too little blood flow to the head. Even migraine headaches can be stopped when this skill is properly developed and applied. To apply it to head-ache control most effectively you would have to get specific information about your particular headaches from your doctor.

It is possible to get instrument feedback about many body functions. Some, of course, are simpler to monitor than others. In addition to temperature, you will find three other useful measures readily available in biofeedback centers in most major cities.

The electromyograph (EMG) measures tension in the voluntary muscles. It is useful in learning to relax in general or in learning to relax specific areas of distress such as the muscles of the head and neck in tension headaches and the muscles of the back in back pain which results from or is aggravated by tension.

The electroencephalograph (EEG) measures brain waves. In different states of consciousness different brain waves predominate. By getting feedback about them one can learn to go into these different states by increasing the various brain waves. Insomniacs can learn to get into states that promote falling asleep easily. Special EEG training has proven effective in helping epileptics prevent seizures.

The galvanic skin response machine (GSR) measures emotional arousal by reflecting the electric conductivity of the skin, that is, how easily current flows from one place on the body to another. The current is so small that it cannot be detected by the person but the scale on the GSR reflects minute changes. The activation of the body caused by a word unconsciously associated with an upsetting event will cause gross movements of the GSR needle. This is the machine that has gained wide use as a lie detector.

You can use the GSR to detect emotional responsiveness so slight you aren't aware of it. This can give you information as to situations that put your body in a stressful state without your awareness. Your body doesn't know the difference between imagined and actual situations so all you have to do is imagine a scene and the GSR will tell you if something upsets you. The GSR is also useful as a measure of hypnotic depth when the suggestion of calmness is focused upon.

There are many other biofeedback instruments which are continually being improved and put on the market for home use. Others are available in hospitals for more complex monitoring. Any of them can be useful in showing you how to develop a different kind of control over yourself. Recall that this different kind of control, allowing rather than forcing, is the essence of hypnosis.

The body gives clear signals about some functions. It is easy to monitor the heart by listening to a surface on which you are lying, by watching the pulse, or perhaps by just listening carefully. Intestinal motility makes itself unavoidably known at times. Hyperesthesia (hypnotically heightened awareness) can make still more functions available.

It is a good idea to end a session with some comment such as, "You will do whatever is necessary for your best health. The knowledge of what to do will come from deep within you, from within your very tissues."

Persist in using every trick to bring about recovery. Expose yourself to stories or experiences of instant healing. Let your imagination go. Suggest that your dreams will lead you to good health. Once health is secured, maintain it with hypnotically induced dedication to good health habits.

Pain

One of the most startling discoveries in the history of hypnosis is the remarkable phenomenon of hypnotic anesthesia. How can something that should obviously hurt cause no discomfort? How can someone lie on the operating table and watch his appendectomy in complete comfort with only the words of his doctor to control the pain?

How this comes about is a question the theorists can continue to ponder. The fact is, it happens, and you can learn such pain control yourself.

Most of my personal experience with anesthesia through self-hypnosis has been in the dentist's office. But one time my ability to induce anesthesia in my hand paid off.

I was working with a new patient in my office at UCLA when I had a most unlikely accident. He was already in a hypnotic state when I decided he would be more comfortable if I raised the footrest of his chair. I told him to continue relaxing as I lifted it. When I reached under to pull it up something very sharp in the mechanism cut into my finger near the root of the nail and ripped the nail up at the cut and away from my finger.

I consciously suppressed a scream with great difficulty, hypnotized myself silently, and got my voice under control without enough time lapse to make my patient suspicious. Then I began talking to him about his hand. At least he thought I was talking about *his* hand. Actually, I was deepening my hypnotic state with hand levitation and inducing hand anesthesia. I got so deep I forgot the patient for a moment and woke up hearing myself say, "The pain is leaving."

He had never been hypnotized before and apparently thought what I had said was normal. At any rate the pain was gone from my hand, and I was able to continue with his therapy for the rest of the hour. The trauma for him came at the end of the session when he saw the torn nail and the dried blood on my hand and arm. He *was* impressed with the power of hypnosis, however.

I wanted to get the wound bandaged up before my next appointment, but the doctor in the employees' medical station insisted that he didn't have the right equipment to take care of it. "Just cut the nail off and bandage my finger," I demanded. He said the nail had to be surgically removed. I started trying to tear it off saying it was simple since I had induced hypnotic anesthesia. He and the nurse were very upset. She wheeled a chair up behind me and the doctor shoved me into it. The nurse pushed me to the emergency room at the other end of the hospital while I complained all the way.

In the emergency room they put me on an operating table and draped me with sheets. It seemed so ridiculous I jumped at a chance to distract myself when some medical students walked by. In a loud voice I said, "I don't need an anesthetic. I've already *hypnotized* myself." When the students heard this they came in to see what was going on.

I demonstrated self-hypnosis to them and lectured from the operating table on the values and uses of hypnosis in emergency room practice. Meanwhile the resident snipped and clipped and bandaged up my finger to which I cheerfully made occasional reference to illustrate the complete effectiveness of hypnotic anesthesia.

I had no pain from that injury except initially, even when it would get bumped. It healed rapidly and left no scar.

The ideal way to handle pain is exemplified in this instance. Several things contributed to my success:

1. Prior practice inducing anesthesia in the hands
2. High motivation to get rid of the pain
3. Opportunity to take time to induce deep hypnosis
4. Reinforcing the anesthesia under ideal circumstances

I learned to induce hand anesthesia my first weekend with self-hypnosis. From then until this incident I had done it dozens of times in hypnosis workshops and seminars.

In this situation I was particularly interested in getting rid of the pain so I could continue with my patient's session. High motivation increases success if the necessary skill is already developed and the motivation isn't compounded by anxiety.

Since I needed to hypnotize him anyway I had a good opportunity to deepen my hypnotic state sufficiently.

Because I wanted to demonstrate the induction of

hypnotic anesthesia to the medical students in the emergency room I naturally took that opportunity to reinforce my hand anesthesia.

Give yourself as many such breaks as possible. Even if you see no immediate use for anesthesia I suggest you hypnotically raise your interest level and learn as much as you can. It is much easier to learn anesthesia *before* the need arises. If you already have chronic or recurrent pain, all the more reason to get busy.

If you give sufficient time and energy, I believe you can learn to induce anesthesia in any part of your body. It is easiest to start with your hand since you have already learned to induce levitation in it. You can use the levitation as a focus to continue inducing other sensations easily.

Hypnotize yourself and spend extra time focusing on your hand before you allow it to rise. When it does float let it move very, very slowly. During the focusing suggest hyperawareness of your hand. Especially focus on the tingling in your fingertips. Once you are clearly aware of the tingling, suggest that it will spread over your whole hand and turn into numbness as your hand rises.

As your hand rises very slowly, focus on the feeling of numbness, remoteness, and hypersensitivity to all sensations except pain. Tell yourself that by the time it has floated up to your face it will have *no* sensitivity to pain.

As your hand is on its way to your face, try various suggestions to facilitate the development of anesthesia. From your experience with eyelid catalepsy and hand levitation you have some idea of the kinds of things that work for you.

Some possibilities are: "The little people who run up to your brain to tell it that your hand hurt are all busy with a party and just don't remember to deliver the message."

"Blue and yellow pipes run from your hand to your head. When the valves are closed off messages can't get through. The yellow ones carry messages of pain. All other sensations are carried by the blue ones. (Go through the process of closing the yellow valves.) No pain messages can get through now. It is impossible for you to feel pain in your hand."

"Pain messages are being diverted into a part of the brain that cannot decode them." (If this type image worked in helping you learn hand levitation or eye catalepsy, elaborate on it now and make use of it.)

"A thick leather glove covers your hand and protects it from pain."

Go through these processes several times, expanding the ones that seem to work best. When you feel pretty sure you have had some effect, test your hand to see if it is anesthetized. Simply give it a pinch. You may be delighted to find that you feel no pain. After you accomplish this, suggest all the normal sensations back into your hand and then induce anesthesia again until you feel confident you can do it whenever you want to.

Once you have this confidence try to transfer the anesthesia to other parts of your body. A good beginning is to suggest that when your hand floats up and touches your face the anesthesia will spread into your mouth.

If you have had chemical anesthesia from a dentist, your mouth is familiar with that feeling and is therefore most receptive. Focus on the sensation of numbness and test by pressing on your gums with your fingernail. Continue this process with other parts of your body as long as it interests you.

If you become discouraged in developing true anesthesia you can do a lot to control pain without it. If you are good at developing a sense of dissociation this can be quite adequate for handling pain. I had my teeth filled for years with no need for novocaine by simply feeling as if my tooth was in the corner of the dentist's office and he was working on it there. Such remote pain is not distressing.

Another possibility is to increase awareness of sensations. This is called hyperesthesia. If you increase all those *except* pain you may be so intrigued by them that the unpleasantness of pain will be overshadowed. If you develop this to a fine art you can pleasantly experience and describe procedures that would normally be excruciating. You will feel the pain but it won't bother you. You will be able to analyze it into its component parts and thus get rid of it through analyzing it away. I know a man who successfully used this technique for abdominal surgery.

With the development of pain control comes the responsibility to use it wisely. Pain serves as a signal that must be responded to for survival. Never neglect this warning. Before you even practice developing anesthesia tell yourself that you will use it to maximum advantage and will never misuse the ability.

If you cannot trust yourself your unconscious will probably take steps to see to it that you are unable to learn anesthesia. We are really much wiser than we give ourselves credit for being. Although you never want to ignore nature's warning signal of pain, you don't need to let the alarm clock ring all day. Once it wakes you up, shut it off.

Pleasure

No doubt your imagination quickly takes off with a heading like "Pleasure." Let it run wild. There are uses you can make of self-hypnosis that only you can conceive. Even if I could think of every possibility I wouldn't know the best approach for you to take in accomplishing it. When you think of something you want to use self-hypnosis for, enhance your determination to do it with suggestions that build confidence and motivation. Then, after experimenting to see what works, design a program to accomplish your desire.

It doesn't matter what you want to do. Maybe you want to learn to draw or paint, write a book, play the guitar, dance, ski, rock climb, fly a glider or a hundred other things. If you have worked your way through all the ideas and techniques up to this point, you have sufficient information and hypnotic skills to tackle anything you want to do. There is only one more idea that I want to add to your repertoire that can be a lot of fun to do and remarkable in its outcome.

It isn't necessary for you to have any philosophical

leaning toward the concept or even to be able to consider it as a possible reality. Your unconscious can certainly accept it, and from the unconscious, talent emerges.

You can use it for just about anything. For example, let's suppose you want to improve your guitar playing but are convinced that you are so nearly talentless that you will never get beyond chording along in one key. After hypnotically raising your confidence and determination and applying the learning techniques you have used, you will quickly find that you are able to play pieces. You will also have an intense desire to play them better. At this point it is time for a superhypnotic technique.

In superhypnosis you develop the belief that in a past life you were a fantastic guitar player. In order to get deep enough to accept this possibility you need to approach hypnotic depth equivalent to the dream state. It is difficult to get that deep while designing a patter for yourself. Therefore, use your recorder to record a big spiel about your other life, long ago and far away. Precede the talk about the person with ten minutes or so of relaxation suggestions and dream-like imagery: floating, drifting, clouds, and so on. You can pick a real person from history or a person that exists now only in your mind. (And in your body, if reincarnation is a real phenomenon and you actually did live this particular life at one time. Every little bit of convincing helps.)

Whichever you do, set the stage, develop the character of this person you were (are), and describe several incidents in which you played your guitar superbly in that life. Use your hypnotically released creativity to design better ways to make the tape but consider some of the following:

"You are the reincarnation of (fill in the name of the guitarist of your choice). You bring with you into this current life the skills and talents you had then. You bring all the perfection of a lifetime of practice. Now that you know you were (name) you will be able to take more advantage of this fact. You can allow your ability to surface into awareness. You will play superbly. You will learn your pieces quickly and easily. You will play perfectly, with expression and deep feeling."

Repeat this suggestion many times in different words. Elaborate the specific ways this past life has affected you to make you a better guitar player. After you finish this part, repeat a number of times, with growing excitement in your voice, that you are filled with enthusiasm and confidence. End the taping with the suggestion that you will now get up, alert and wide awake and play as you have never played before.

If you can believe this message for even a few moments it can be very helpful in giving you confidence in your ability to make the most of the talents you *do* have.

Now, before you close this book, take a deep breath, look way up, and let your eyelids slowly close down. Deliberately relax your body. Let go completely. And as your body relaxes, as your mouth opens, as your head falls over, let all the thoughts pour out of the top of your head, leaving your mind empty and quiet. Allow the wisdom deep within you to well up, develop awareness of the personal power you have; the power to do whatever you want and need to do, to become the way you want and need to be. Rest assured that you have all the talent, skill, and ability that you can ever need, right within you. Then with a complete feeling of confidence, let your eyes open and begin to do what you need to do.

Index

DR. FREDA MORRIS is a licensed psychologist in the state of California and practices privately in Berkeley. She studied clinical and experimental hypnosis at the University of Chicago and taught its use in psychotherapy as a professor of medical psychology at the UCLA Medical School. Dr. Morris has taught workshops for the Society of Clinical and Experimental Hypnosis and for the American Society of Clinical Hypnosis and is a member of the American Society.